CW00602351

THE SPICE
OF LIFE

THE SPICE
OF LIFE

The memoirs of
The Rt. Hon. Lord Renton
P.C., K.B.E., T.D., Q.C., D.L.

With my best wishes

David Renton

THE
SPICE
OF
LIFE
By David Renton

Copyright © David Renton

David Renton has asserted his right under the Copyright, Designs and
Patents Act 1988 to be identified as the author of this work

A CIP catalogue record for this book is available from the
British Library

The photographs in the book come from family albums, and it has not
been possible at this stage to trace the copyright position. No copyright
infringement is intended. If there are any questions on copyright, please
contact the publishers.

Design and artwork by Paul Holder
Email: p.holder@ntlworld.com

and published by
Calder Walker Associates
PO Box 60, London SW15 5WS

Printed by Bell & Bain
Scotland

ISBN: 0-9541275-3-6

FOR MY DAUGHTERS, CAROLINE, CLARE
AND DAVINA

ACKNOWLEDGEMENTS

The Spice of Life would never have reached manuscript stage without the help of Morag Scott-Ferrar who painstakingly transferred my earlier drafts on to the computer over many hours. I would also like to thank Betty Hunt for spending many hours hunting for old photographs and memorabilia, Lulu Appleton for her helpful editorial suggestions, Paul Holder for typesetting and designing the book and Alan Gordon Walker of Calder Walker Associates for his involvement and commitment.

My thanks and love, as always, go to my daughters Caroline and Clare whose encouragement ensured this memoir was published.

(Photo © Ken Challenger / The Hunts Post)

FOREWORD
BY THE
RT. HON. SIR JOHN MAJOR
K.G., C.H.

Of all the men I know, David Renton is among the most remarkable. He has served longer in the Houses of Parliament than, perhaps, any man in history. He was elected a Member of the House of Commons in 1945 and served for thirty-four years, and at the time of writing, has subsequently served a further twenty-seven years in the House of Lords.

Nor is he a passive politician. David is always involved. In the Commons he held senior Ministerial posts and in the Lords he remains active at the age of ninety-seven. David is still a man bubbling with enthusiasm over everything that happens, and more inclined to look at tomorrow than yesterday.

But his memoirs inevitably look back.

He remembers his father marching off to war in 1914; a career at the Bar; serving in the Second World War; Churchill's last Government; a Ministerial career; decades of work on behalf of those with learning disabilities; and life in the House of Lords.

His memoirs are rich in anecdote of a world now gone, and laced with insight and wisdom. Historical figures are brought back to life by his pen.

I was David's successor as M.P. for Huntingdon and, from the moment we met, a friendship began that I will always cherish. Even so, I learned more about David from this book. His life threads through nearly all of the twentieth century, and the beginning of the twenty-first.

Such lives are rare. But then – in many ways – so is David Renton.

22nd May 2006

ILLUSTRATIONS

Front cover: Photo © Baron Studios.

Back cover: Photo © Cambridge Evening News.

CONTENTS

(Photo © Lord Crathorne)

INTRODUCTION

After a long and varied life, including sixty years in Parliament, I have been persuaded by my family and by friends, to write about my life whilst I am able to remember most of it.

It has certainly been varied: my forebears, education, practice at the Bar, Army life, travels, pastimes and Parliamentary and charity work have each been remarkably varied. "Variety is the spice of life": hence the title of this book!

I hope that I have not been a "Jack of all trades and master of none", and I cannot claim to have known "something of everything and everything of something", as Francis Bacon advocated (and) should be the aim of a good education. Winston Churchill maintained however that: "a change of occupation is as a good as a rest", which has also been my experience.

I have been luckier than I deserve with wonderful parents, a blissfully happy marriage and good daughters and grandchildren. Some of the events I have witnessed over the years have been momentous, and I have known as friends some of the leading people who have shaped our country's destiny in the twentieth century. Above all, in spite of heavy responsibilities, some setbacks and two world wars I have vastly enjoyed life.

If this book encourages the rising generation, and gives you, dear reader, some interest and amusement, I shall be thrilled.

Thank you to my family, friends and colleagues and also to John Major, who succeeded me as M.P. for Huntingdonshire after thirty-four years, for writing the preface to my life story.

CHRONOLOGY

1868 29th December	Father born at Macduff, Banffshire
1885 28th November	Mother born near Georgetown, British Guiana
1907 2nd September	Parents married in London
1908 12th August	I was born at The Bridge House, Dartford, Kent
1913 September	Started kindergarten at St David's School, Hextable
1914 4th August	England declares war on Germany
1914 22nd August	My father goes to France as Major RAMC. Mother follows him there a few weeks later as a VAD nurse.
September **1914** to March **1916**	I go to kindergarten at St Bride's School, Helensburgh
1916 March	Parents return from France and I rejoin them and return to St David's School
1917-1922	Preparatory school at Stubbington House, near Fareham, Hants
1922-1927	School House, Oundle, Northants
1927-1931	Read law at University College, Oxford – M.A., B.C.L.
July/August **1928** and **1929**	Studied French at *cours des vacances,* Grenoble University

July/September 1930	Studied German at Ferien Schule, Bonn University September
1931 to June 1932	Pupil in solicitors' office, Great Western Railway
1933 26th January	Called to the Bar, Lincoln's Inn
October 1932 to July 1933	Bar pupillage with G. O. Slade
October 1933 to June 1939	Bar practice at No. 3 Paper Buildings, Inner Temple, in chambers of Roger Bacon
October 1938 to June 1939	Circuit Junior, South Eastern Circuit. Elected to Bar Council
1938 June	Commissioned as R.E. officer in the Territorials. Transferred to R.A. in August 1940 during Battle of Britain
1939 3rd September	Britain declares war on Germany. I was called up a few days previously on mobilisation and served in the Army throughout the war.
1st January 1940 to March 1941	Staff Lieutenant 29th AA brigade, Coxtie Green, Nr Brentwood, Essex in Battle of Britain
March 1941 to March 1942	Staff Captain 28th AA Brigade at Topsham, Nr Exeter, Devon
April 1942 to January 1943	Staff Captain, 18th AA Brigade (anti-tank and anti-aircraft) serving in Egypt and Libya, attached to the 8th Army
1943 January/February	Hospitalised at Alexandria – Sick leave in Luxor and Aswan
March 1943 to April 1944	Served in G.H.Q., Cairo as Major
1943 September	Hospitalised again in Cairo

April **1944** to May **1945**	President of the British Courts of Tripolitania, and Deputy Legal Advisor to British Military Administration
1945 End May	Flew home with a view to being chosen as candidate for Parliament
June **1945** to May **1979**	M.P. for Huntingdonshire (thirty-four years)
1945 October	Returned to Bar practice in Chambers of Eric Sachs Q.C., with Quintin Hogg
1946 September	Member of Parliament Delegation to Austria
1947 17th July	Married Paddy Duncan at St Margaret's, Westminster
1948 22nd November	Caroline born
1950 23rd August	Clare born
1951-1952	Delegate to The Council of Europe, Strasbourg
1954 April	Queen's Counsel
1954 13th September	Davina born
July **1954** to December **1955**	Deputy Chairman, East Kent Quarter Sessions
1955 August to September	Visited USA and Ontario for the Automobile Association
1955 December	Parliamentary Secretary, Ministry of Fuel and Power
January **1958** to July **1962**	Joint Parliamentary Under-Secretary of State, Home Office
1961 May	UK representative at first event Conference of European Ministers of Justice, Paris
1961 May	Minister of State, Home Office
1962 July	Ceased to be a Minister and became a Privy Councillor
1962 Early September	Led Parliamentary Delegation to Morocco
1962 Late September	Resumed Bar practice at No. 5 Kings Bench Walk

1963 January	Bencher of Lincoln's Inn
January 1963 to December 1968	Recorder of Rochester
1964	Made Knight of the British Empire
1964-1967	Deputy Chairman, Essex Quarter Sessions, Chelmsford
1965 September	Member of Parliamentary Delegation to Australia
1966-1968	Part-time Commissioner of Assizes (relief Judge) at the Old Bailey
1968-1971	Recorder of Guildford
1968 September	Member of Parliamentary Delegation to Guyana
1971 November	Acquired Livingstone House, Kirkcudbrightshire from cousin Harry Lockhart-Mure
1971-1974	Member of the (Kilbrandon) Royal Commission on the Constitution
May 1973 to May 1975	Chairman of the 'Renton' Committee on the Preparation of Legislation
1978	Retired from practice as Q.C.
1978-1982	Chairman of MENCAP and then President
1979	Ceased to be M.P. for Hunts (succeeded by John Major). Became Treasurer of Lincoln's Inn
1979 June	Given Life Peerage
1980 January	Visited India with Paddy
1980-1990	President of Statute Law Society
1982-1988	Deputy Speaker, House of Lords and President of MENCAP
1986 24th April	Paddy died
1998	President for Life of Conservative Peers Association
2005	Resigned as President of Conservative Peers Association

CHAPTER 1

THE DOCTOR'S SON

I was born on the "glorious" 12th August 1908, at The Bridge House, Dartford, Kent, where my father practised as a doctor and surgeon from 1903 until he retired in 1947. He was Dr Maurice Waugh Renton, a Scot. My lovely mother was Eszma Olivia, née Borman; her father had been a sugar planter in British Guiana and her mother was a daughter of the first British Pasha.

Myself with my mother, Eszma.

The Bridge House, Dartford, Kent where I was born.

1908 was a good vintage year. It also gave birth to the Territorial Army, the National Farmers Union (NFU) and the Scout Movement, each of which I joined, the Borstal System and the Probation Service to which I sent offenders, as well as the Court of Criminal Appeal, before which I sometimes appeared!

Across the road from the Bridge House was Holy Trinity Church, where I was christened David Lockhart-Mure Renton: David after my paternal grandfather and Lockhart-Mure after my maternal great-grandmother, whose family property, Livingstone in Kirkcudbrightshire, my family now own.

My Godparents were varied and ecumenical: a canon of the Church of England, a Roman Catholic priest and my father's eldest sister, Aunt Jeannie, who was a Scottish Presbyterian. At that church, which dates from Norman times, and was rebuilt in the early fourteenth century, the principal tomb is that of a German called Spielman who came to Dartford as the first person to make paper in the British Isles. King James I granted him a monopoly for producing plain paper of a size that is still called foolscap. He chose Dartford because the River Darent, which flowed through our garden and alongside our house, had a constant supply of pure water. As a boy I used to catch eels and coarse fish in its pure and plentiful stream.

The Bridge House had been a doctor's house from early in the eighteenth century. Although it lay in the old part of town at the foot of East Hill, it had a spacious garden with a grass tennis court. One had only to walk beside the river past the vicarage garden to be in the countryside. I was an only child and worshipped my parents and I had a very happy childhood. The Bridge House was my home until I married in July 1947.

My father was one of the first to own a motorcar in Dartford and one of my earliest memories was motoring from Kent to Cornwall for a seaside holiday in August 1913. My father drove the car, which boiled over on every steep hill, as most cars did in those early days, and so we had to carry a big can of water to replenish the radiator. Once one got away from built up areas, the roads had no tarmac surfaces and were dusty in summer. There were not many other cars and if my father saw another car ahead of us raising a lot of dust, he had to decide whether to close up and blow the horn and overtake it, which was often difficult, or to hold far back so that we did not get covered in dust and choked with it. The journey took three days and when driving my father sometimes let me sit between his knees and steer the car, at the age of five! That is now a criminal offence.

That autumn I went to a kindergarten called St David's, at Hextable, a journey of three miles which, with four children of professional men at Dartford, was undertaken in an open trap pulled by a self-willed pony and driven by a rather drunken old man. On one occasion when crossing Dartford Heath the pony decided to leave the road to have a drink at the water fountain on the grass verge; the trap overturned and we all fell out. One of the boys, Arthur Carter (another doctor's son) had a jar of tadpoles, which spilt onto the grass, and he was more worried about losing them than about tumbling out of the trap! It was at St David's that I had my first lessons, but I was not quick to learn – I was a late developer academically.

CHAPTER

2

THE
FIRST
WORLD
WAR
1914-1918

On the day I was born in 1908 *The Times* leading article had referred to the private visit of Edward VII to his first cousin, the Kaiser. It said: "The meeting of the two sovereigns is a benefit not only to their own Empires, but to the world at large, since the greatest interest of every nation is peace, and those who promote peace dispense a blessing in which every friend, whether of Great Britain or of Germany, will participate."

My father had served in the South African War as an army surgeon where he made a splendid collection of photographs, some of them pretty gruesome, of men lying dead. Horse casualties were very heavy. I can remember him showing me his photos soon after my fifth birthday in August 1913 and I asked him if there would ever be another war and he replied, "War is so horrible that I don't think there'll be another one."

A year later the First World War started, Germany invaded Belgium and on 4th August we declared war on Germany. At the time my parents and I were on holiday at Macduff in Banffshire, my father's birthplace. We joined the crowd in the centre of Banff, the small country town on the other side of the River Deveron, and saw the muster of the Territorial Battalion of the Gordon Highlanders, who marched in small groups from nearby towns and villages. Each group had a piper or two – they were a brave and merry sight and we all cheered them as they arrived. Their Colonel, John James George (one of my father's oldest friends, a local solicitor and a jolly man) returned salutes with a broad grin on his face. His great grandson, the late Robin Cooke, M.P. became my PPS at the Home Office forty-five years later and was one of the greatest experts on the Palace of Westminster. He was knighted in 1979.

As my father was on the Reserve of Officers of the RAMC (Royal Army Medical Corps), we travelled south by train next day for him to report to the War Office where he was told that the British Army had enough doctors, so he was asked if he would form a forward casualty unit to be attached to the French Army as they were short of medical personnel. He soon persuaded several of his medical friends to go with him to France, as well as some motorists to drive and maintain ambulances.

My father was my hero and I did not like the prospect of him going to war. He and his army colleagues left No. 1 platform at Victoria Station towards the end of August 1914. When my mother and I had waved him goodbye, I was very upset and my mother said: "Don't worry, dear! The war will be over soon, and Daddy will be home for Christmas." But I was not to see him again for nearly two years. After his departure, to cheer me up, my mother took me to the London Zoo for the first time, where to add to my troubles, I was scratched in the face by a jealous monkey.

The next time I stood on platform No. 1 at Victoria Station was on 20th October, 1958 when, as Parliamentary Under Secretary of State for the Home Office, in the Home Secretary's absence, I was presented by the Queen to old 'Papa' Theodor Heuss, President of Germany, making the first official visit to this country of a German President. For me it was a strange turn in the wheel of fortune.

In September 1914 my mother left to join my father's medical team in France as a VAD nurse. Before she left she took me to Helensburgh in Scotland where I attended the kindergarten of St

Greeting the German President at Victoria Station, 1958.

Bride's Girls School, of which Aunt Jeannie (my father's sister) was the first head mistress. She owned one of the houses for girl boarders and I, aged six, was the only boy living there. It was a well-patronised school; Bonar Law sent his daughters there and among those who attended the kindergarten were John Logie Baird, who invented television and Jack Buchanan, the glamorous musical comedy star. In my youthful 'go about' days I used to boast that I had been to the same girl's school as Jack Buchanan!

With the war on we were told that patriotism, loyalty and courage were what mattered most in life. On the wall of the school assembly room were photographs of George V, Queen Mary, Admiral Jellicoe (whose son succeeded me as Minister of State at the Home Office in 1962), and General French. Each day at assembly, after prayers, we had to turn towards each of them in turn and say "good morning!"

Early in 1916 my mother returned from France and then brought me home to Dartford where I returned to St David's as a weekly boarder. In 1916 the Zeppelin raids on London had started and these vast and vulnerable airships flew above the River Thames. Searchlights shone onto them and I saw two brought down in flames by RFC (Royal Flying Corps) fighters - very thrilling!

My father had had a strenuous time in France, especially after the casualties in battles like the Marne. Besides doing a vast amount of surgery, at which he was highly skilled, the French put him in charge of an advanced field hospital in a small chateau and of a base hospital at Fort Mahon near Boulogne. It was there that in early 1916 he contracted double pneumonia, brought about by the awful weather on the Western Front, and was consequently invalided out of the army. When he had recovered he returned home and resumed his practice in Dartford. It was wonderful for me to have him home again and he at once set about seeing what needed to be done for my education and improving my physique, which was not as good as it should have been.

He gave me my first bicycle which I loved to ride fast downhill. One morning in the summer of 1917 I tried to jump my bike over a brick and fell hard and injured my left knee, where I still have a scar.

On the same afternoon I secretly had my first flight in an RFC aeroplane! On Dartford marshes, less than a mile from my home, there was a RFC Aerodrome, and that summer the officers had an open invitation to come and play tennis on our grass court. I asked one of them if he would take me up in an aeroplane – he agreed but said I was not to tell anyone. He told me to leave my bicycle at a certain spot and crawl under the barbed wire where he would be waiting for me with a biplane: an Avro dual trainer. He put me in the back seat and said I could hold the joystick, but not to force it against his movement of it in the front seat. Taking off for the first time was a great adventure - at first there was a wonderful feeling of speed, but when we were about 400 feet above the ground we seemed to be crawling slowly through the air. However, it was lovely to see the Thames, the River Darent, the Church, my home and all the countryside I was so familiar with from the air. One week later, in July 1917, I was in hospital having my appendix removed.

CHAPTER 3

STUBBINGTON
1917-1922

In September 1917, aged nine, I started prep school at Stubbington House, near Fareham, Hampshire. It had a great naval tradition and had in those days produced more Admirals and Victoria Crosses (VC's) than any other prep school. Two of our contemporaries won the VC in the Second World War: Admiral Capel Miers, the submarine hero, and Captain Shelton Agar.

Captain Scott of the Antarctic had been there and I became obsessed with the story of his tragic expedition to the South Pole and read every book about it in the school library. His son, Peter, the great bird artist and naturalist, joined the same house and same class as me at Oundle and we became lifelong friends – he was always losing his pencil and borrowing mine!

The discipline at Stubbington was very strict; games were important and until the war ended we were taught mainly by old men and middle-aged women. The school was owned by Colonel Montagu Fraser, who after his return from the war preached a sermon every Sunday on the theme of unselfishness and the need to help others.

They discovered at prep school that I had an audible voice (due to my father's deafness in one ear) and some talent for recitation and acting. In my letters home, nearly all of which my mother kept, there are frequent references to recitation and the performances I gave in school plays and at concerts.

In the summer of 1919, after the end of the war, there were many garden parties in and around Dartford to raise funds to help the returning soldiers. Lloyd George had said that men should return to 'a land fit for heroes', but the provision made for them was pitiful. At those fund-raising events I was put in front of large audiences to recite Kipling, John Oxenham and other patriotic poets, and always received more applause than was good for me. This caused my mother to try and stop me from getting swollen-headed - she was always afraid that these early successes would lead me to a career on the stage.

At Stubbington I learned to play cricket and in my last year was in the First XI. In August 1919 my parents and I went to Hythe for our summer holiday and one day my father took me to see Kent play Yorkshire at Dover, which thrilled me and cricket became an obsession with me – so much so that although I did not display an especially good memory at my work, I was able to remember without effort the scores made by Kent players and many other first class statistics. However, I did also memorise the dates of all our monarchs from 1066 onwards and still remember nearly all of them to this day!

While at Stubbington my parents applied for places for me at Winchester and Oundle, the only two schools that had special entrance exams, which I thought was a bit hard bearing in mind my mediocre academic ability. However, I did manage to scrape into a low class at Oundle. So did Joe Simpson, who later became Commissioner of the Metropolitan Police, while I was an Under Secretary of State at the Home Office, but I had no influence on that decision!

I was a sickly child and before my eleventh birthday I had already had chicken pox, measles, whooping cough, German measles, influenza and had had my appendix and adenoids removed. Although my parents were tall and well built, I was rather small for my age and this worried them. In order to expand my chest further my father suggested that I learn to play the bugle in the Scout Band at school and this was the only musical instrument I ever mastered. I completely failed to learn how to play the piano, mainly because the woman who taught me sat there with a ruler with a sharp edge and rapped my knuckles every time I played a wrong note.

Although I was in the First X1 at cricket, I was no good at football or athletics, but when I went and presented prizes at the Stubbington Sports Day in 1959, three weeks before my fifty-first birthday, to my astonishment I won the old boy's race! It was a 100 yards handicap and the previous night I had been dancing with my wife at The Pegasus Ball in the Temple until three in the morning! I had overcome my early problems with health and now at the age of ninety-seven I am lucky enough still to be quite physically fit. I played cricket for the Lords and Commons Cricket Club until age sixty-six and tennis until I was ninety, I also hunted until I was seventy and kept a horse until I was seventy-five.

CHAPTER 4

OUNDLE
1922-1927

As soon as I passed into Oundle in 1922, my parents went and saw the famous 'Sanderson of Oundle' – the Headmaster – who had made it into a great science school. They got on well with him and he decided to have me in his School House. He died, alas, in the summer holidays and so when I went there in September 1922 Dr Kenneth Fisher, who had been a science master at Eton, had been appointed the new Headmaster. He was a considerable scientist and sportsman and very kind but firm.

At Oundle they made us work hard, play hard and sing lustily for the performance each year of one of the great religious choral works which were an important feature of life there. I continued to act in school and house plays and to play cricket. Like all other boys, I joined the Officers Training Corps, which was supposed to be voluntary, but in fact every boy in the school joined unless his health was not good enough. I played the bugle again!

Oundle was the first of the leading public schools to teach science in a major way and as my father wanted me to join him in practice as a doctor, most of my work was aimed there. I went onto the science side for my last three years, did what is known as the first year of medicine - physics, chemistry, zoology and botany - and got a medical vacancy to

University College, Oxford. Peter Scott also did the same subjects but went to Cambridge.

Oundle produced many flying men, including two Atcherly brothers, one of whom won the Schneider Trophy and broke the air-speed record in about 1930. They both became Air Marshals. In School House we had three MacRobert brothers, each of whom was killed flying in the R.A.F. Their mother then presented a fighter aircraft to the nation in memory of them – it was named 'MacRoberts' Reply'. John Grimston, who in 1947 became my brother-in-law, was also in School House and at Oxford, where he joined the University Air Squadron. In the war he was in the Air-Sea Rescue Service, flying mostly over the Atlantic. That great horseman Harry Llewellyn was in School House too, as was his eldest brother Rhys.

THE PSYCHOLOGICAL MOMENT

In the summer term of 1926 on Sunday afternoons I wrote a one-act play in two scenes called *The Psychological Moment*. It was about a doctor's son who fell in love with the daughter of a rival doctor. The doctors disliked each other intensely and both of them tried to prevent the son and daughter from marrying, but love was too powerful. When the doctors drove their cars by chance towards each other in a very narrow Kentish lane, where neither would reverse to get out of the way, one of them at last broke the impasse by saying, "We can't go on like this; our young people won't let us!"

The play was performed in the summer holidays at Joyce Hall, Betsham – the home of our dear and closest friends the Snelling-Colyers, before an audience of about forty people. Everyone enjoyed it, mainly because it was not difficult to recognise some of the characters portrayed. It took me at least an hour's writing to produce lines that took about three minutes to act. I decided I would never write another play.

In my last year at Oundle I became a school prefect and got my school colours for rugby-fives and house colours for cricket; in my last term I had the choice between being captain of the shooting VIII and

Senior Fives at Oundle, 1926.

training for Bisley, or captain of the third XI at cricket, which I chose and greatly enjoyed.

I made many friends at Oundle and was sorry to leave. It was and is a first rate school and in our day won more Higher Certificates (equivalent of A-levels) and University Scholarships in both arts and sciences than any other public school, even Winchester.

Years later I found that the following simultaneous office holders in Huntingdonshire were old Oundlians; the Lord Lieutenant (Ailwyn, Lord de Ramsey), his predecessor (Denis, Lord Hemingford), the High Sheriff (John Goodliffe), the County Coroner (John Davies), the chairman of the Conservative Association (The Hon. Anthony Finch-Knightley) and the M.P. (myself). Mere chance – not an old boy network!

CHAPTER

5

OXFORD
1927-1931

During the long holiday between leaving Oundle and going up to University College Oxford in October 1927 to read medicine, it dawned on me that I would never be as good a doctor as my father, especially in surgery, at which he was so highly skilled and experienced. After consulting my mother, I decided to tell him that I wished to read law instead and become a barrister. He was upset about this and tried to change my mind because he wanted me to go into partnership with him, but I knew that my work as a doctor would compare unfavourably with his.

Therefore, on my first morning at 'Univ' I went to see the Senior Tutor and told him that I wished to read law instead of medicine – he was shocked because the Dean of the Faculty of Medicine was a don at the College, and I had obtained a precious place there to read medicine. He asked me to see him next morning for his decision and when I did so he stood there, his face wreathed in smiles and he told me he had persuaded Dr C K Allen, the Law Tutor, to take me on as an extra pupil.

My first set of rooms at University College had the distinction of having been occupied before the war by the Russian Prince Youssoupoff, the man who killed Rasputin.

I enjoyed reading law. At the end of my third year I got a second in Jurisprudence, in spite of the fact that the superb C K Allen had become Professor of Jurisprudence and so was no longer my Tutor. My supervision in that final year was divided between T H Taylor, the blind law tutor at Balliol, who was a remarkably fine tutor, and Archie Campbell, who, after obtaining five firsts at Glasgow and Oxford, had become Law Tutor at University. To answer even a simple question, he went into a trance and spent anything from five to fifteen minutes telling one everything that was known on the point.

'Univ' had a great legal tradition dating back to the late eighteenth century when Lord Elson was Lord Chancellor, and his brother Lord Stowell was President of the Court of Admiralty. They were 'Univ' men and so have been many famous lawyers since, including Gordon Hewart, who when he was Lord Chief Justice in the 1930s wrote *The New Despotism*, which was a damning criticism of the growth of bureaucracy and of government by decree. My first Tutor, C K Allen, wrote two other critical books – *Law in the Making* and *Law and Orders*.

When in 1973 I was asked by the Heath Government to preside over the first enquiry for a hundred years into our methods of drafting Acts of Parliament, to endorse how it should be done – also known as The Renton Report – I felt that it was in the well established University College legal tradition.

My friend Kenneth Diplock, who became a persuasive Law Lord, was a contemporary at 'Univ' and became a constituent of mine and a hunting companion. In 1930 I became President of the Eldon Society, which was our College Law Society.

At Oxford I began to take a close interest in politics and in my third year became President of the University Liberal Club. I regularly attended the Union, which was great fun. Many famous men came as guest speakers to both the Union and the Liberal Club, including Churchill, Birkenhead, ex King George of Greece and John Simon. Paradoxically, as did many others at the time, I thought that Sir Oswald Mosley, who was in the Labour Government at the time as Chancellor of the Duchy of Lancaster, was the most striking orator of them all. It later became clear that his vanity was fanned by his oratory as he tried to become a dictator and spent the Second World War incarcerated for his fascist beliefs.

In the general election of May 1929, when I was Secretary of the Oxford University Liberal Club, I organised for our members to speak in support of Liberal candidates in Oxford and neighbouring constituencies. I found myself a somewhat ordinary speaker compared with my contemporaries in the Club such as Derek Walker-Smith, Arthur Irvine and Jim Mallalieu, who were fluent and overflowing with words and ideas and, like me, became M.P.s in 1945. Conservatives at Oxford at that time included Quintin Hogg and John Boyd-Carpenter, both of whom became very close friends of mine and ministers in Conservative governments.

In 1930 John Boyd-Carpenter and I decided that we should have a joint meeting of the Conservative and Liberal Clubs, of which we were respectively President, and to invite the first woman M.P., Nancy Astor and A P Herbert to debate 'temperance.' We booked the Union debating hall for the occasion and arranged a large dinner party there. Both speakers accepted, but alas Alan Herbert was struck down with flu at the last minute, so we simply had a talk by Nancy Astor and she answered questions from the audience. She was strident and amusing, but vicious in her attacks on several well-known public figures who enjoyed a tipple. As two of them had their sons in the audience this was embarrassing for me as I was in the Chair and really felt that she was overstepping the mark. Several people walked out, but this did not deter her – indeed she indicated that she had touched a soft spot, which seemed to please her!

At Oxford I played cricket in summer and rugby and rugby-fives in winter. Although I did not really excel at any of these games, I enjoyed them thoroughly and sometimes played for the University at rugby-fives and for my College at cricket and rugby.

In order to get some riding, of which I had been very fond since early childhood, I joined the Horse Cavalry Squadron of the University OTC. Our horses were an odd assortment and I discovered that the one which I liked best and which jumped best was accustomed to pulling a milk float in ordinary life. Our training was done in a riding school with a tan floor in winter and on Port Meadow in summer, where we mounted drill and manoeuvres. For our annual camps in July we went to Tidworth on Salisbury Plain where we were attached to regular horse cavalry regiments – the King's Hussars in 1928 and the King's Bays in 1929.

At the second of those camps our Troop Sergeant was Duncan Sandys, who was very dashing. As there was a bright moon on our last night it was decided to go on night manoeuvres and our Troop had as its objective the capture of Salisbury Hill on Salisbury Plain – a large grassy hill with a clump of trees. Although we were not supposed to go any faster than a steady trot, when we got to the foot of the hill Duncan collected his horse and shouted "Charge!" and broke into a fast gallop up the hill, but none of us knew that at the top there was an ancient British vallum, (which means a sudden dangerously deep drop.) He reigned in his horse just in time to stop and raised his arm and shouted, "Halt!" We rode back to our base at a very slow trot and none of us mentioned the incident to the officers, but several of the horses were slightly lame the next morning.

The Masters of 'Univ' were diverse and interesting. When I first attended Chapel in 1922 the aged previous Master, Prebendary Carlyle, took the service and prayed for 'our gracious Queen Victoria!' Sir Michael Sadleir was Master throughout my four years, an august but remote figure who was less interested in the College than in his work as chairman of the Oxford City Education Committee. One day however, the Dean asked him to speak to two undergraduates: one was Thompson, an old Etonian, who was captain of the College Boat, which had done well on the river and he had to be congratulated upon it; the other was an obscure fellow who did no work and should be warned that if he did not pull himself together, he would be sent down. So the Master summoned them both to his study the next day, Thompson went in first and was greeted with the words' "Sir, you are a disgrace to the College!" In those days we addressed the Dons as 'Sir' and they sometimes addressed us as 'Sir', especially if they had to rebuke us.

When I was there, that delightful man John Redcliffe Maud became Dean, and thirty years later he became Master, having meanwhile held a number of important public appointments, including Permanent Secretary to the Ministry of Fuel and Power. When I was appointed Parliamentary Secretary there in 1955, he greeted me by saying, "I had to put up with you *in statu pupillari* but all is forgiven now that you are one of my masters!"

My father generously allowed me to have a fourth year at Oxford to take the BCL, although continuing to enjoy myself tremendously with games, politics and college life.

During two of my long vacations I went to France in the hope of improving my French, which was an interesting and useful experience, although I have never been more than a very ordinary linguist. In August 1928 when attending the *cours de vacances* at Grenoble, I came nearer to death than I have ever been in peace or wartime. Whilst descending alone from the top of Chamechaude (2087 metres) I lost my way and fell down about twenty metres onto loose scree at the top of a ravine. A boulder fell against my head but did not knock me out. I managed to stop my fall about fifteen metres above a sheer drop of 600 metres, scrambled to the top of the ravine and was helped down the mountain by the *Eclaireurs*, French Scouts.

At 'Univ' we had a Literary Society called The Martlets of which I became President, but not because I had any literary merit. I enjoyed the meeting and annual dinners and the only paper I remember giving was on 'De Quincey, The English Opium Eater.' Stephen Spender, who was in our year, came to the meetings and already showed some promise as a litterateur, but had not begun to take life as seriously as when he became famous – he was rather a giggler then!

I made many friends at my College – especially among my fellow cricketers. We formed a team called 'The Utopers' to play a few matches each summer against the surrounding villages of Oxford at weekends. In some summer vacations we had a week's tour in Dorset - where we stayed at Weymouth. 'The Utopers' were a cheerful lot and included several really good players from other colleges, including Ian Peebles who played for England.

My best friends at Oxford (apart from John Grimston – who became my brother-in-law when we both married two of the lovely Duncan sisters and he later became the Earl of Verulam) were John Boyd-Carpenter, Brian Davidson and Patrick Hamilton. Strangely enough we had all been at different public schools, were in different colleges and read different subjects – they were all Tories and I was a Liberal and we were all interested in politics, tennis and bridge. John Foot (the third of the four famous brothers, which included Michael) was also a good friend and great fun – he remained a Liberal and then became a Life Peer.

All good things, it seems, must come to an end and Oxford was a happy and fruitful experience. 'Univ' was a delightful old College and produced some bright people among my contemporaries, including several High Court judges. At the age of eighty-one I was elected an Honorary Fellow – an unexpected honour, which I now share with ex-President Clinton. However, there is a difference between us – I was there for four years and took two law degrees, including the BCL - he was there for two years, did not take an exam and was told not to return to College! He was made a DCL by Diploma, which just proves there is no justice!

I always disliked exams, mainly because I write so slowly and as a result had difficulty in answering the questions fully enough in the time allowed. Although I scraped through, I never got a first. Looking back it seems to me that too much emphasis was placed on exam results – people who got firsts do not always become high flyers.

CHAPTER

6

THE BAR
BEFORE
THE WAR

I came down from Oxford in June 1931 and decided to use the time between then and September by going to Germany to learn the language – and to see a bit of that country and its people. Hitler had already had his putsch in the beer cellar at Munich, there was serious unemployment and inflation, and although President Brüning had become reasonably successful at stabilising the situation, there were serious undercurrents of discontent. I went and stayed with Herr Doktor Engerov and his wife and three children at Bonn-am-Rhein for about six weeks, having prepared myself by studying a German grammar book. He was Professor of English at Bonn University, his mother was English and he was bilingual, which for me was a disadvantage for he preferred to get up to date with English idioms and slang by conversing with me in English rather than by making me speak German. However, at weekends I explored the town and countryside on my own, which I greatly enjoyed, especially several short trips up the Rhine on steamers, which had brass bands on board. One Sunday I got up early intending during the day to walk up each of the Siebengebirge (seven hills) on the other side of the Rhine. I walked up two hills in the morning and then arrived at a restaurant at the top of a third, where I had a very good lunch – washed down with the only red hock, which was called 'dragon's blood'. This made me incapable of climbing more than one other hill that day!

One weekend two friendly young Germans, seeing that I was alone, asked me to join them, and later we did several excursions together and became very friendly. They were unemployed and had little money and they predicted that Hitler would come to power and that it would be good for Germany. I argued strongly against them, speaking German, but I was quite unable to convince them that they were wrong. We corresponded for a few months after I returned to England, but I assumed that when Hitler came to power, they probably joined the Hitler Youth out of sheer desperation. About fifty years later I met a man called Bill Kerruish in my Huntingdonshire constituency whose mother was English and his father German, and for a time was in both our Territorials and the Hitler Youth organisation, until he became disgusted with it. He wrote a remarkable book about his experiences before and during the war called *The Broken Swastika*. His wife became Chairman of one of our Conservative Branches in Huntingdonshire and one of their sons became an Equerry to the Prince of Wales.

In early September 1931, after I had been in Bonn for about six weeks, my mother came to join me and we went to Munich and Salzburg for the first time – and loved both places. We enjoyed our excursions together to Hohenschwangau and Neuschwanstein in the foothills of the Bavarian Alps, and to various places round Salzburg. I acquired a taste for Austrian waltzes and for wiener-schnitzel and salzburger nockerl, a marvellous soufflé.

On the way home we visited Mainz for a couple of days, and one evening we were attracted to a restaurant overlooking the Rhine, where we heard jolly music being played inside. We wandered in for dinner – and found that a German regimental reunion was taking place. The men were not in uniform but were wearing medals, including several with iron Crosses. Their families were with them. As soon as I realised what sort of gathering it was I said, "Let's go!" But we were intercepted and put at a table on which very soon a small Union Jack was placed, and those officers who spoke English came up to us and were friendly and, with their characteristic formal politeness they gave us a warm welcome, bought us wine and invited us to join them in the evening's proceedings, which consisted mainly of singing various German marching songs that we did not know. When the evening became rather hectic with lots of clinking of glasses and linking of arms, we quietly paid our bill and slipped away. It had been a fascinating experience.

THE GREAT WESTERN RAILWAY

My Uncle Allen Borman's brother-in-law was Frank Hoskins, a solicitor who was parliamentary Agent to the GWR (Great Western Railway) and the only lawyer in the family. He strongly advised me to become a pupil in the solicitors' office of the GWR, overlooking the roof of Paddington Station, before going to the bar, and so in September 1931 I started a most useful experience there, which lasted ten months.

After a week or two a general election was called by Ramsey MacDonald, at the head of the newly formed National Government. My father was President of the Dartford Liberal Association, and he and I agreed that it would be better if the Liberals (who had no chance of getting a candidate elected) were to support the Conservative candidate; after much discussion in the Committee of our small Liberal Association they agreed to support him. He was a delightful man called Colonel Angus McDonnell, the brother of the Earl of Antrim. In the Dartford area they were not accustomed to Irish blarney, but they fell for him completely and he was duly elected. I was a supporting speaker at several of his meetings, and my father took the chair at some of the more important ones. The National Government won with a huge majority and unemployment, which had doubled in the two previous years under the minority Labour Government, was halved during the following three years.

At Paddington I was a pupil in the room of the GWR's High Court Solicitor, in which capacity I found myself helping in the briefing of Walter Monckton K.C. and W S Morrison, both of whom appeared fairly often for the GWR and other railway companies. Sometimes the work would take me to South Wales, where there were some controversial cases of negligence against the railway, in which its employees displayed their unquestioned loyalty to the Company by giving evidence strongly in its favour, whatever the merits of the case. Then and ever since, I have always enjoyed the company of Welsh people, even though I have never had much in common with them, except that my Christian name is David. Their charm, sense of humour, quickness of mind and fine voices always appeal to me.

The unemployment and economic depression at that time were very hard on the people of South Wales, and it was tragic to see so many pale, thin and hungry looking men standing about in the streets, especially in the mining valleys.

CALL TO THE BAR

Although, having read Law at Oxford I was exempt from most intermediate parts of the bar exam, I had to take the bar finals, which I eventually did without distinction, while still at Paddington. There is a rule that one cannot be called to the bar within six months of being a pupil at a solicitor's office. Therefore I could not get called until 26th January 1933. I had been a student of Lincoln's Inn since 1929, and had eaten the requisite number of dinners – namely twelve yearly for three years. My sponsors had been my first tutor, C K Allen and Professor Sir William Holdsworth, a family friend of ours known as 'The Hogger', the Vinerian Professor of the Laws of England, of which he wrote the history in nine volumes.

PUPILAGE

In October 1932 I became one of the five pupils of Gerald Slade, at No. 1 Brick Court in the Middle Temple. He had one of the busiest junior practices at the bar and although he had so many pupils, he was a most conscientious pupil master. When a set of papers came in, the clerk would hand it without delay to one of us and tell us how soon we should have a draft pleading, opinion, etc., ready for Gerald to take home and correct when he had read the instructions. The day after he had done so, the papers would be handed to one of us with a note saying when he would discuss our draft. He was a great master of the art of drafting written pleadings, and each of us owed him a tremendous debt for what he taught us.

When I had been a pupil of his for six months and had still not begun to practise, the GWR sent me my first brief, which was an unopposed petition in the Chancery Division to take out of Court some money deposited there by the GWR when promoting a private Bill in 1908, the year I was I was born. The petition was heard by Mr Justice Eve who, I suppose because it was unopposed, wanted to give me a chance to impress my clients, so he asked me a number of quite unnecessary questions to which the answers were obvious. I did not hear again from the GWR until a year later, when they started briefing me regularly.

MY VARIED PRACTICE

In October 1933 on the advice of W S Morrison, I started practice at No. 3 Paper Buildings - on the second floor, in a small set of chambers just being started by Roger Bacon, a junior with a growing High Court practice of good quality.

For the first three months no work came to me, but I had joined the S E (South East) Circuit and the Kent Sessions, both of which I attended hoping for a dock brief, which never came. In January 1934, however, some Dartford solicitors briefed me to prosecute in five cases at West Kent Quarter Sessions at Maidstone, which was the start of a regular flow of work in West Kent until the war started. In March 1934 the GWR started briefing me to appear in Traffic Commissioners' Courts all over their system, and I had the good fortune to appear in North and South Wales and at Birmingham, Bristol, Exeter, Truro, Plymouth, Dorchester, Hereford, Newport, Taunton, Yeovil and other places. These visits not only brought a steady if modest income, but also enabled me to see and learn about interesting and sometimes beautiful places in Wales and the West Country for the first time. Although, being on the S E Circuit, I was an intruder when appearing against members of the local South Wales bar, I was never made to feel so; such is the generous spirit of the bar that I was always given a good welcome, especially in South Wales – where they produce such talented and spirited advocates.

I had a variety of experiences when doing this work. On one occasion in a remote and beautiful little town called Bargoed, in the Snowdon Peninsular, my opponent was an elderly local solicitor – the brother of David Lloyd-George, Prime Minister during and after the First World War. Sometimes when appearing for the railway in remote towns in the Welsh valleys, I would be the only person in court who could not understand Welsh; but the Traffic Commissioner was A T James, a delightful Welsh K.C., who would rapidly size up the situation in the case, question the witnesses himself in Welsh and then tell me what was happening, explain the point at issue and ask me if I had anything to say on behalf of the railway. I would then argue my case, which he would translate into Welsh, causing some generally pungent rejoinder, and then he would smile broadly at everyone in court and give a compromise decision with which nobody could reasonably quarrel.

In a case in Cornwall, when a road haulier was applying to carry pigs a hundred miles or so to Exeter, when it was normal practice to send them by rail, I asked the applicant why they could not continue to go by rail, and the answer came: "Well, you see, it's like this, the little pigs begin to fight – and then it frightens the other passengers!"

One summer's evening after dinner at Dorchester, I decided to go for a stroll outside the town and was attacked by a swarm of enormous hornets, and ran for my life back to my hotel where the chase ended as the hornets had retreated.

The other three mainline railway companies sometimes had cases in which they were jointly interested with the GWR in opposing applications for bus or coach licenses; and in this way I came to be briefed by all four of the main line railways. However, I always leaned against becoming a specialist at the bar and I am glad to say that my practise in Kent and on Circuit also gradually grew, and I began to get a variety of work in all three divisions of the High Court. In those days at the bar, there was much less specialisation than there has been in the past forty years.

Three cases illustrate the more interesting side of my varied practice. The case of In re Conley was an action for fraudulent preference in the Chancery Division, in which Roger Bacon and I appeared for the receiver in bankruptcy of a fur dealer. He had obtained credit at Lloyds Bank and Barclays Bank on the strength of personal guarantees given by his wife and mother. With those credits he obtained large overdrafts for purchase of furs from traders, to whom he paid deposits of only part of their value. He then sold the furs profitably, used the purchase money to pay off overdrafts, thereby releasing his wife and mother from their personal guarantees, but failing to pay the fur dealers the balance of the purchase money owing to them. They sued him but he was unable to pay, and one of them made him bankrupt. On behalf of the creditors we sued the wife and mother and each of the two banks, alleging that they had been fraudulently preferred with full knowledge of the circumstances, with the result that the other creditors had suffered loss. Against us two Kings Bench juniors there was a great array of talent: Fergus Morton, K.C. and Cyril Radcliffe, K.C., who became Law Lords, W N Stable, K.C., one of the editors of *Williams Bankruptcy*, John Buckley (a specialist in that branch of the law) and others - the cream of the Chancery Division. However, Roger Bacon's skill and persuasiveness carried the day, and Mr Justice Farwell found in our favour against the wife, the mother and the banks, and said that they were jointly and severally liable. They all appealed, but after the Court of Appeal had given them a thorough roasting by the end of the first day's hearing, they asked us if we would settle and they agreed to our rather stringent terms as to costs.

In the King's Bench Division I was in the case of GWR and LMS Railway v. James and Hodden, in which some traders who did big business importing and exporting through the ports of Bristol, Avonmouth and Portishead, were sued by the two railway companies for a declaration that they were entitled to increase charges for carrying iron ore and other heavy goods from those ports to factories in the Midlands. Walter Monkton K.C. led Alfred Tylor and me for the railways, and Stafford Cripps K.C. led Lionel Heald for the plaintiffs. There was a lot of money at stake, but the technicalities of the case are not interesting. For me the fascination of it was to see how Walter and Stafford, who were both great friends and effective adversaries against each other, conducted their cases in very different ways. Both of them had complete mastery of the facts, the law and the issues - Walter was gently persuasive and charming, and with sweet reasonableness made our case appear to be unanswerable. But Stafford was didactic, tense, destructive, masterful and just as convincing in his different way. Mr Justice Porter found in our favour and our opponents decided to appeal. By the time the appeal was heard Walter had become deeply involved advising King Edward VIII in the Abdication Crisis, but this did not prevent him from arguing our case successfully in the Court of Appeal, where it was fought to a finish on somewhat narrow legal issues.

In the Divorce Court in the case of Roberts v. Roberts & Chown, I was for Mrs Estelle Roberts, a famous spiritualist medium, who was the respondent in the divorce case brought by her husband. He named as co-respondent her solicitor and business manager, Tilson Chown, with whom she was alleged to have committed adultery. Mrs Roberts was accustomed to filling the Albert Hall and other big places to overflowing with her spiritualistic séances, from which she earned large sums. My roommate at Paper Buildings, Jack Samuel-Gibbon, appeared for Tilson Chown, and we were both led by a remarkable character, Tommy Carthew, K.C., who was the first Lt Colonel of the regular army (outside the Judge Advocates' Department) to become a K.C. He was one of the early fighter pilots in the RFC and the first man to take the Prince of Wales (later, briefly, King Edward VIII) up in an aeroplane.

The petitioner, Mr Roberts, had spent months shadowing his wife and Tilson Chown in their travels about the country, while she earned her living as a medium and, on occasions, he even climbed up trees and lamp-posts in the hope of seeing them commit adultery in upstairs bedrooms in hotels and boarding houses. His case depended mainly on his own evidence. The defence was that his wife and her business manager were drawn together by their common interest in spiritualism and had never committed adultery. As Tommy Carthew had become interested in spiritualism when his first wife died, we could not have had a more suitable leader. Mr Justice Henn-Collins had also been interested in it but had not become personally involved.

When Mrs Roberts gave evidence, she explained that she was the medium in this life of a Red Indian Chieftain called 'Red Cloud', who had been dead for two thousand years. In her trances she lay on her back and spoke in a man's deep voice. It was, she said, the voice of 'Red Cloud'. On hearing this, the Judge asked the pertinent question, "Does Red Cloud speak English? To which the witness gave the answer "I speak English when I go into a trance, and express the thoughts which he puts in my mind." The case lasted about a week, and on the second and third days Mr Chown arrived at Court with plenty of bank notes to pay our refreshers. These were the takings of Mrs Roberts' séances the previous evenings. Our clerks very properly told him that the money should be handed to the solicitors who had briefed us, and not to our clerks or to us. The judge found in favour of Mrs Roberts and Mr Chown, and poor Mr Roberts, who had led a lonely life for several years, was very upset. Afterwards Mrs Roberts gave each of us a copy of her book about her experiences as a medium.

In October 1938 a firm of London solicitors, who for years had had business clients in Germany, instructed me to draft statements of claim in the King's Bench Division in two cases on behalf of the Deutsche Bank against Jewish refugees in England. I was reluctant to act in these cases, but we have a rule at the bar that we are obliged to accept instructions from solicitors in cases within our line of practice, so long as they are credible and we are likely to be paid. This is known as the 'cab rank' rule. In June 1938, being pretty sure that there was likely to be a war against Germany, I had joined the Territorials, and the cases had still not come to court when the war started in September 1939. My clerk had meanwhile insisted on immediate payment for each piece of work I did, and I never heard about the cases again. When the war started they were taken over by the custodian of Enemy Property.

THE CIRCUIT JUNIOR

Having gone Circuit pretty regularly since 1934, I was elected Circuit Junior of the S E Circuit commencing 1st October 1938. The Junior is in effect the secretary and the adjutant of the Circuit, and it involves a fair amount of administrative work, especially as ours was the largest Circuit – covering the counties of Norfolk, Suffolk, Cambridgeshire, the Isle of Ely, Huntingdonshire, Hertfordshire, Essex, Kent, Surrey and Sussex. The job is unpaid and involves one in some expense, but it has the advantage that when judges have the chance to nominate a member of the bar for a poor prisoner's defence brief (as it was then called), the Junior, if present, was the person to whom the brief was given by the court.

Also, one was twice a year briefed by the Director of Public Prosecutions in more important cases, in which a leader was also briefed, including the occasional murder case.

In March 1939 the Circuit held a large Dinner at the Café Royal to celebrate the appointment as High Court Judge, of the then Leader of the Circuit, Jimmy Cassels, K.C. and Roland Oliver, K.C.; the Lord Chief Justice - Gordon Hewart - came as our guest. As Junior, it fell to me to reply to the speech which he made in proposing the toast of the Circuit; with some trepidation I made a speech in which I thanked him for honouring us with his presence, and for enlivening us with his wit, and added "but I must remind the Chief Justice by misquoting his own works, that it is important not only that he should have dined well but that he should manifestly be seen to have dined well." As Hewitt was a rotund *bon viveur*, who always looked as though he *had* dined well, this caused the members of our Circuit great merriment and prolonged laughter; but Hewart did not like it! Next day an unfortunate young barrister, when addressing him in the Court of Criminal Appeal, quoted the well-known phrase, "It is important not only that justice should be done, but that it should manifestly be seen to be done," Hewart thought that this was a put up job in order to cause him further annoyance, which was very bad luck for the young man as he had not been at the dinner and knew nothing about it!

In the spring of 1939 I was elected to the Bar Council, in pursuance of what is known as the 'under seven years' rule', which ensures that a number of junior members of the bar with short experience became members of the Council. At the several meetings which took place before the war came in September 1939, I was mainly concerned to protect the interests of those of us who had joined the Territorials and who would be called up if war came. It was agreed that we should receive half fees for any of our cases in which we had done the preliminary work, but were unable to appear in court due to war service and therefore had to have another member of the bar appear on our behalf. This arrangement worked well enough at first, but after about a year those who were serving found that the cases in which they had been previously involved in the early stages had all been tried without their getting any reward.

In July 1939 I attended Norwich Assizes, and in the Bar Mess in the Royal Hotel in our private dining room some of us had a keen argument over dinner. Gerald Howard, then a prosecuting Counsel at the Old Bailey, Stephen Lycett Green, John Boyd-Carpenter (who had become my Assistant Junior) and I had a fierce argument about Neville Chamberlain's performance at Munich. I was the only one in the Territorials and therefore knew how badly prepared we were for war, and I considered that his decision at Munich to delay our declaration of war was essential to gain us another year for preparation; but I had to withstand the onslaught of the others, who criticised Chamberlain heavily.

At those assizes I defended three poachers on the Sandringham Estate, whose total bag in the early hours of the morning the previous February, was one rabbit. The defence was that they did not know they were on private property. They were found guilty and I made a strong plea in mitigation, but the newly appointed judge, Roland Oliver, was determined to make an example of them and they were given rather stiff sentences.

During those years before the war I worked hard at my practice, but enjoyed life too - I loved tennis, golf, shooting, dancing and the theatre, and had plenty of each of them. Two things worried me: the tremendous difference between the standard of living of the well off and others, their education and their prospects, and the threat of a Second World War. In spite of unemployment and poverty, there was very little crime. Although there was no national health service, people did not lack medical and nursing attention when they needed it, but they often did lack dental treatment. There were plenty of large hospitals - local authorities ran some and others were voluntary hospitals run by charities. My father was a prosperous doctor and surgeon who charged his patients only what they could afford, but did most of his operations without being paid for them. He and his partners approved of the panel system, under which most wage earners paid a few shillings a year to a doctor as a form of medical insurance. My father often found that the bad housing of the day caused much of the ill health.

CHAPTER 7

THE SECOND WORLD WAR 1939-1945

Major Renton, 1945.

THE BATTLE OF BRITAIN

I was commissioned as a sapper subaltern in June 1938, three months before the Munich crisis, (during which we were called up and served for a fortnight). In mid-August 1939 I went on our annual training with the 322 Search Light Battalion, Royal Engineers. It took place on the Isle of Grain, near Rochester and on 24th August, on general mobilization, we were ordered to our war stations, which were in the area between Dartford and Rochester on the South side of the Thames, to a depth of about five miles. Our Company Headquarters were in our drill hall at Horn's Cross. Another subaltern, Jack Temple, and I were luckily given the grounds of Wombwell Hall near Gravesend, which belonged to our friends the Colyer-Fergussons, as our Section H.Q.

In moving from our training area in the Isle of Grain to our new section area, which was covered by half a dozen searchlight sites, a huge cable on a drum failed to arrive at our war station. There was a tremendous row about this, and later a formal inquiry was held. The cable was never found, which was quite serious because it was worth several hundred pounds and was a vital part of our operational equipment. Jack and I quite expected to be court martialled but were able to show that we had taken all reasonable precautions. Its disappearance was an unfathomable mystery. Our explanations were accepted, and we got on with preparing for war.

Sunday, September 3rd 1939 was a cloudless, warm and lovely day, with the temperature in the seventies. We all turned on our radios before 11 a.m. to hear the Prime Minister, Neville Chamberlain, declare war on Germany in a short, dramatic speech. As soon as it was over the air-raid sirens sounded all over South East England, and the sky was quickly full of our aircraft travelling wildly in all directions and at various heights. We had not by then acquired much skill in aircraft identification and we assumed that all this excitement meant that German aircraft had already come to bombard us. At our small H.Q. we therefore manned our old Vickers machine gun and ordered those men who had rifles to have them ready loaded. Our headquarters cook was preparing the Sunday lunch and so I ordered him to hand his rifle to me. I was itching to fire at a low-flying German aircraft – which never came. Enquiries were later made by the R.A.F. as to what had caused a false alert of the approach of enemy aircraft. It transpired that some wild geese in East Kent had been mistaken on the radar for enemy aircraft! Eventually the all clear went in time for us to enjoy our Sunday lunch, taken *al fresco* in the brilliant, warm sunshine and we enjoyed our first wartime meal in peace.

That autumn became known as the period of the phoney war. There were no serious air raids, only occasional reconnaissance aircraft. The British army in France and Belgium were able to take up their war positions without much effort. However, the anti-aircraft searchlights and guns had to be at the ready all the time, especially at night. And so Jack Temple and I spent most nights visiting our six searchlight sites, which we also sometimes visited in the daytime, when we would hear the men's complaints about food and their sleeping quarters, check equipment, arrange leave rosters and hear about their problems at home. As they all lived locally and had largely been employed in peacetime in cement factories and paper mills in North Kent, their family problems were much more easily dealt with than one found later when serving abroad.

Shortly after Christmas 1939 I was told to report on 1st January 1940 to Brigade H.Q. in Kensington, where I was to become Staff Lieutenant. Our Brigadier was a splendid man, Kenneth Ian Gourlay, D.S.O M.C., and his wife too was delightful and had the regular officer's wife's flair for getting on well with people. As the winter had become pretty rough, with lots of snow and ice, I must confess that I did not mind being ordered to work in the comfort of Kensington. It was also my introduction to the British army's well-established administrative methods. The warrant officers and N.C.O.'s at Brigade H.Q. were all regular soldiers, who considered that they knew exactly what to do, which was to save officers from doing anything, and I found that instead of having to dictate letters myself, they prepared them ready for me to sign. I was appalled by the style of English that was used, and I fear that

I must have caused some offence by saying that I would prefer to have letters first shown to me in draft – instead of ready for signature. Fortunately, when the Brigadier heard about this, on receiving a complaint from the senior warrant officer, he supported me, and all went quite smoothly after that.

When we had been in Kensington for a few weeks, an interesting case left over in my junior practice was set down for trial in the King's Bench Division of the High Court, and I asked the Brigadier if he would allow me to appear for a few hours in court each morning and afternoon, provided that I worked through the evenings on my administrative work. Again I had that splendid leader, Tommy Carthew, K.C., (who had led me in the spiritualist's divorce case) and as I had done all the preparatory work before the war started, I reckoned that with Tommy's help the arrangement would work well. When the Brigadier asked me why I wanted to do this case while the war was going on, I said "Well, it will last several days, and with luck it will double my income for the year!" Being a shrewd Scotsman he at once agreed to let me do it. It was a case in which we appeared for the Plaintiff, who was suing the Kent County Council and one of their doctors who had treated a patient negligently in an isolation hospital near Dartford marshes. These cases always involve a lot of dispute on the medical details and turn largely on the evidence of expert medical witnesses called by each side. Tommy did it superbly and we won the case. When I went back to the mess that evening the Brigadier – on hearing the result – said, "Renton will pay for all the drinks this evening", and it turned into an expensive party which almost wiped out my refresher fee for the last day in Court!

Our Brigade area covered the whole of Kent, Essex and Suffolk but excluded Greater London. In the early summer of 1940 our H.Q. moved to Boxted House, north of Colchester, and we spent that glorious summer there working hard in pleasant surroundings near Constable country. The German onslaught against the French, Belgian, and British armies had meanwhile got under way in the spring; and then in late August the Battle of Britain began, and our anti-aircraft guns were frequently in action by day and by night, and our searchlights were a great spectacle as they lit up the sky every night. In late 1940 all anti-aircraft battalions of the Royal Engineers were converted into Royal Artillery Regiments. On what became known as Battle of Britain Day, 15th September, which was one of the most crucial turning points of the war, an elderly Rear Admiral, who was Naval Officer in command at Harwich, came and had lunch at our H.Q. He was a fine old salt with a beard, who had seen service all over the world and had a tough time in the First World War. We all talked about the war situation at home and abroad, and he concluded that conversation by saying. "Well we know that whatever happens, we shall never be beaten – because we're British!" Brigadier Gourlay agreed laconically merely by saying, "Obviously". That night hundreds of German aircraft passed overhead on their way to bomb London docks and the East End.

A fortnight later Jean Gourlay, his pretty, blond daughter, was married to a Wing Commander in the R.A.F. in the 600 year old church at Little Horkesly, a mile or two from Boxted. As the best man had just been killed flying in the Battle of Britain, I was asked to stand in for him. It was nevertheless a happy wedding on a lovely day, and the reception was held at our Brigade H.Q. That night the first magnetic mine dropped by parachute completely destroyed the ancient church and the village pub opposite it; and it was a solemn thought that the happy wedding that afternoon was the last that would be held there. It was also an ill omen, for the bridegroom was killed a few weeks later flying over France. The mine had noisily exploded at about bedtime, and Douglas Courage, our Brigade Major, and I collected several of our men and went by car to see if anyone needed help. Our main concern was for the people in the pub, who luckily had escaped injury although the building was destroyed. We found them trying to rescue the pigs, which they kept at the back of the building, and which were a pathetic sight, obviously suffering from shock. Owing to the blackout there was not much we could do, but we were able to arrange for the people at the pub to be given shelter in neighbouring houses.

During a weekend leave in October 1940 I played golf with my mother one afternoon when several hundred German aircraft flew high over us on their return journey after bombing London. My father walked round with us. The aircraft started dropping their unspent bombs and my tall old father, who was strolling back to the club house, was knocked over by the percussion of a bomb which exploded thirty yards behind him on hitting a fairway. It made a crater, which was turned into 'Renton's bunker'.

In November we again moved our H.Q. - this time it was to a beautifully built large modern house in the Georgian tradition at Coxtie Green, four miles north of Brentwood, and almost next door to Pilgrims Hall, the home of my 'Univ' friend, Bill Lawrence, who had followed his father and grandfather as a partner in the solicitor's firm of Lawrence Graham & Co, of Lincoln's Inn. It was Bill's eldest sister, Lesley Lewis, who wrote that remarkable book, *The Private Life of a Country House*, describing the country life of Pilgrims Hall between the wars.

Soon after we had settled in at Coxtie Green, we were playing bridge one Sunday evening with the Brigadier during an air raid, when we heard a bomb descending on us with a long, loud whistle, obviously from a great height. We dived under the dining room table for shelter, and waited for the worst. However, the bomb fell in the garden about forty yards from the house, penetrating the earth for about thirty feet, and did not explode and we resumed our game of bridge. In war there are long periods of boredom between spells of too much excitement, so bridge helps quite a lot!

On 1st January 1941, I was sent on the three-month Anti-Aircraft Command Staff Course at Garston Manor, near Watford. As this was only five miles from Gorhambury, near St Albans - the home of my Oundle and Oxford friend, John Grimston, I spent the short weekend leaves there every other weekend. As the shooting season had been extended for a month that year owing to the wonderful showing of pheasants and the need to produce more food, I had some splendid shooting with John, his father, the Earl of Verulam and his two younger brothers, Brian and Bruce, who both lost their lives as pilots in the R.A.F. later in the war. I had first visited Gorhambury in October 1938, after the Munich crisis, and on various occasions after that. It is not only an historic and elegant Taylor house, with probably the best and most expansive collection of family portraits from the fifteenth to the twentieth centuries, but there was also wonderful hospitality and many parties where people of all ages enjoyed themselves on equal terms. My visits there played a great part in my life, for I eventually married Marjorie Grimston's youngest sister, Paddy Duncan, although I did not meet her until after the war.

DEVON: 1941-42

The Staff Course was well run, imaginative, realistic, and enjoyable and at the end of it I surprisingly passed with the comment, "well above average for the course." I then returned to Brigadier Gourlay's H.Q. in Essex, but within a week or two I was appointed Staff Captain of 28th A.A. Brigade, which covered Exmoor, West Dorset and the whole of Devon, except Plymouth. The Brigadier rejoiced in the name of Coward (which made Douglas Courage laugh) and he had been the T.A. Colonel of the Searchlight Regiment, which covered most of Essex. I discovered that he had applied for me as his Staff Captain, not so much because I had managed to pass Command Staff Course but because he thought that I would help to make a bridge four! The Brigade Major was Michael Berry, later Lord Hartwell, who became Editor-in-Chief and Chairman of the *Daily Telegraph* in 1954. He was a man of great efficiency and determination - a workaholic, but who was capable of relaxing in the mess and had great charm. The Intelligence Officer was no less a personage that Lieutenant Clifford Dupont, who was a London solicitor before and after the war, until he migrated to Rhodesia - where after UDI, he was appointed President Elect. The Staff Lieutenant was a remarkable character called Francis Ellerton, who had served in the First World War and was a London businessman and a keen sportsman. He had acquired a pack of beagles which he heard was about to be dispersed, and we got permission from the Divisional H.Q. to keep them at our Brigade Headquarters at New Court, Topsham, near Exeter, to feed them and provide Army transport to and from the meets, as it was considered that this was suitable recreational training for the troops. And so we had some most enjoyable early morning hunts on foot in the lovely, hilly East Devon countryside.

During that summer of 1941 there was not much air activity over our huge Brigade area and so the Brigadier decided that we should visit each of our Regimental Headquarters in turn and carry out formal inspections as required by King's Regulations. He let me have a number of dates when these should take place, at the rate of one a week, and told me to make the arrangements with the adjutant of each regiment.

On the day appointed for the first of these inspections, to a Regimental H.Q. in a remote part of Dartmoor, the Brigadier and I got our batmen to polish our buttons, and we made ourselves look as smart as possible. We then set out in his car which carried his flag on the bonnet, and drove nearly twenty miles, only to find when we got to the H.Q. that there was no sign of life at all, except a rather sleepy bombardier on duty at the gate. I jumped out of the car and asked where the guard was, whereupon the man looked blankly at me and said, "What do you mean, Sir?" I then asked him if he realised that the Brigadier was carrying out an inspection, and the man said he knew nothing about it; so we drove in, found that there was just a subaltern there as a duty officer, and that he also knew nothing about the inspection. I then got out my pocket diary, which revealed that I had brought the Brigadier along exactly one week too soon! I fully expected a fierce explosion when I admitted this, but he made me feel rather worse by being frightfully kind and forgiving about it.

The rest of the programme had to be cancelled, however, because we were suddenly told that about a thousand Dunkirk veterans were being sent to our brigade for rehabilitation and re-equipping, and we had to spread them among our units after carrying out elaborate documentation procedures.

Throughout the winter of 1941-42 we had a very busy time – we had six regiments of artillery and searchlights and other units spread over a wide area, and at the Brigade H.Q. there were very few of us to do the work. Court martials were time consuming and so were the apparently endless, traffic accident reports. Strangely enough the man who had the most car accidents was called Gunner Careless!

As we were only a few miles from Tiverton, I was able to spend the occasional weekend leave at the home of my Oxford friend, Pat Heathcote-Amery, where we exercised his horses and did a bit of rough shooting. His mother had a tragic life: losing her husband in the First World War, her eldest son in a flying accident in the 1930's and Pat was killed in 'the box' at Bir Hachem in the Western desert in 1942. Finally her youngest son was killed in the battle of Normandy. She lived until she was ninety – her great consolation was the beauty of their seventeenth century, stone-built house and lovely garden at Chevithorne, near Tiverton and the memories of her brave husband and three sons.

On one occasion I was driving from Exeter to Chevithorne and was about three miles out of the town when I saw a young VAD walking with a suitcase in the same direction I was going, so I stopped and offered her a lift, to her parents' home near Tiverton. She was Anne Chichester - we became friends and when she was posted away to some distant hospital she lent me her horse, which I kept living rough in a field at Newcourt. One day before taking a ride, I was picking out its feet; it was standing on rather soft ground and lost its balance, giving a tremendous lunge, and its hind foot came down on my instep with an awful crack. It hurt like the devil and I thought I had broken every bone in my foot, but I was lucky and although my foot swelled so much that my riding boot had to be cut off, an x-ray a few days later revealed that I had broken no bones at all. The swelling went down, the severe bruising receded and it has never troubled me since. The moral of the story is: 'Never try and pick out a horse's feet when it is standing on soft ground!'

Luckily for me it was the only injury I sustained throughout the war, and I think, partly as a joke, the Brigadier insisted that I should complete an injury report, have it signed by the M.O. (Medical Officer) and forwarded to the Divisional H.Q. at Bristol. The Divisional Commander, Major-General 'Tiny' Allen, who was tall and cheerful, visited our H.Q. a few days later and with feigned concern said that he had come to visit the wounded officer!

EGYPT AND LIBYA: 1942-45

Having volunteered for overseas duty, in early March 1942 I was ordered to report to the Royal Artillery Base Depot at Woolwich. When I got there I found that I was the first 'item' in the formation of a new artillery brigade. I was given a book containing 300 other 'items', the first of which was to apply for a batman, then a lance-bombardier clerk, then a typewriter and stationery, then various other – mainly technical - personnel and finally active service equipment for all concerned, for both temperate and tropical climates. Approximately the 280th 'item' was to apply for a Brigade Major and so John Brocklebank arrived and we became lifelong friends. He had played cricket at Eton, Cambridge and the Gentlemen, and if the war had not intervened, he would have gone on a MCC overseas tour as a spin bowler. He belonged to the shipping Brocklebanks, whose firm was the oldest in the country having been started at Liverpool in the eighteenth century by a sea captain. Years later, in the family tradition, he became chairman of Cunard.

At last everything was ready for 'item' No. 298, which was a Brigadier! We were assigned Brigadier Beynon, a charming man who had been an army friend of my father in the First World War, but sadly he failed his medical and was replaced by Brigadier 'Barmy' Morton. He suffered from gastric ulcers and carried a tin of biscuits with him everywhere. When I told him I had arranged for him to have a medical examination by an army doctor, at Woolwich, he said, "Oh don't bother, I have a friend who is going to examine me." Thus he was passed for overseas service, in spite of his ulcers!

Eventually all the 'items' in the book were ticked off and we sent a signal to the War Office saying that we were ready to be sent overseas. Nothing happened for a fortnight, then we were put on forty-eight hours notice, but when it expired we still had not received any embarkation orders and so we waited again. This happened a second time, but finally towards the end of April it was the real thing and we were put on a train to Liverpool. I had said my fond farewells to my devoted parents at Dartford three times!

On arriving at Liverpool we went straight on a board a fine modern passenger ship, The *Andes*, which had been built in the 1930's for South American cruises. When we got on board we found out at last which were to be some of the regiments in our brigade and, as we had suspected, we were prepared for a mobile anti-tank and anti-aircraft role in the Middle East. In fact ours was one of the two big convoys which were the build up for the battle of El Alamein. Altogether there were two thousand officers, men and nurses on board our ship. The officers slept in comparative comfort – eight or ten to a double cabin. The N.C.O.s and men slept mainly in hammocks, and in crowded conditions, on the lower decks which in peacetime would have been used to carry cargo. However, the catering – both for officers and men – was good and there were plentiful quantities of liquid refreshment of all kinds on board.

The journey from Liverpool to Durban lasted five weeks, and we were well protected by the Royal Navy against submarines, which were lurking all over the ocean. Our first and only port of call between Liverpool and Durban was Freetown in Sierra Leone, which had a fine natural harbour spacious enough to accommodate most of our convoy. We were not allowed ashore, and after waiting there for five days we sailed out late one evening. As it was very hot I took my mattress up on deck to sleep under the stars – I awoke at dawn to the thrilling spectacle of our ship flanked on either side by *HMS Nelson* and *HMS Rodney* – the two largest battleships in the world – gleaming in the tropical sun. It made one feel very proud and seemed to epitomise what Churchill had called "the might, majesty, dominion and power of the Royal Navy."

When we first crossed the equator in mid-Atlantic after leaving Freetown, the traditional ceremony was organised. Old Major Maskell, our signals officer, was ordered by the Brigadier to be King Neptune; I was made Clerk of his Court and told to write the script. The ceremony took place one afternoon at the side of the ship's swimming pool and was great fun as I had been told to be as rude about everyone as possible in my script. I was particularly rude about Colonel Peter Heber-Percy, the C.O. (Commanding Officer) of one of our regiments, who at the end of the proceedings pushed me into the pool, still wearing my makeshift lawyer's garb!

To avoid submarines, our convoy sailed two hundred miles south of Cape Town and kept well out to sea in the Indian Ocean. Even so there was a moment when the most colossal floating mine appeared just in front of us. Apart from a destroyer ahead, we were at that stage in front of the convoy – the destroyer signalled a rapid warning to us and our navigator took swift evasive action and we were able to miss it by a few yards. A machine gun on deck was ordered to fire at it, but this did not detonate it and the following ship had to use a Bofors gun to get rid of it.

On arriving at Durban we were sent ashore for a glorious fortnight, where our Brigade H.Q. slept in some comfort in a requisitioned hotel and the officers were made honorary members of various clubs. The flat racing season was in full swing and dances were arranged for us, at one of which I met a pretty blonde and I invited her to dinner two nights later, but she could not come because she had to go into hospital, so I visited her there and took her some flowers. When I told them in the mess about my disappointment, somebody said, "He couldn't get a girl into hospital more quickly!"

We did several excursions to the interior in hired buses, including a most interesting one to The Valley of a Thousand Hills – a native reserve about 1,000 feet below sea level – it is an eerie place of volcanic origin, full of rocky pinnacles and extinct volcanoes and one of the hottest places in the world. The local Africans still lived in little round huts, which were surprisingly cool inside.

Eventually we left Durban, but the rest of the journey was on a large old French passenger ship called *L'Isle de France*, which was most uncomfortable and had no proper supply of fresh water. What little there was ran out when we were on the way up the Red Sea. On the last night of our journey I again slept on the boat deck, and when I awoke in the morning it was to see the sun rise and light up the red hills of the Sinai Peninsular, which divides the Gulf of Akaba from the Gulf of Suez; a fine spectacle.

On arriving at Suez in great heat, we were put onto a train which went across the Eastern desert to Tel-el-Kebir, where the British had routed the Egyptians in 1882. We stayed there under canvas for a few days and we were ordered to tie our revolvers, and the men their rifles, to our wrists at night for fear they would be stolen by locals creeping around the tents at night. Our next move was to Heliopolis, where we set up our Brigade H.Q. in a villa and our regiments were deployed to various defensive positions in the Delta. We were, at that stage, under the command of British Troops in Egypt, whose H.Q. was in one of the big hotels overlooking the banks of the Nile. There was little enemy air action, largely owing to the Americans arrival in the Middle East, where their air forces combined with ours gave us superiority in the air. The 8th Army had retreated to El Alamein, where the line was firmly held, and most of our work was in preparation for the battle preceding the advance, which eventually took place on 23rd September.

Meanwhile I had the pleasure of getting in touch with various cousins in Egypt. My great uncle, Charlie Borman, lived in a spacious flat above the British Consulate in Cairo with his son Walter and three daughters. My mother's first cousin Bertie Rickards lived in a villa at Ramleh, East of Alexandria, with his six children, including his daughter Pearl, who was a smashing blonde. He was head of the Foreign Criminal Investigation Department of Alexandria City Police, and they kept open house for their British friends.

At last our Brigade was given the signal to move our H.Q. owing to the impending start of the Battle of El Alamein, so we moved to Alexandria and nearly all our heavy artillery, which had been idle in the Delta, was moved to El Alamein to take part in the 8th Army's barrage which started the famous battle, the biggest artillery barrage in history. The noise was deafening and lasted for about six hours. I wondered how so much ammunition could have been assembled in the desert seventy miles from anywhere. The battle itself raged for three days with heavy casualties on both sides, and when the Germans decided to retreat, it was the signal for our forward units to advance. Our brigade had to wait until Mersa Matruh was captured several weeks later and then we made our H.Q. there in the only habitable ruin, which was the small Lido Hotel, at the edge of the big natural harbour. It was a lovely little seaside town, the most westerly in Egypt. In the desert nearby there was a massive ammunition and equipment base of the Italian Army.

We were provided with salt water soap (one piece between about six of us) and had a much needed wash in the harbour bay, which had a gently sloping beach.

The Germans and Italians had left Mersa Matruh in a bit of a hurry, but before doing so they had fouled every possible place where men could shelter and on the sands. This caused a terrible stink and our troops became infested with disease carrying flies. I suffered from one of my bad sore throats and completely lost my voice. There had been a lot of diphtheria, and as I was showing the symptoms, I was sent to hospital soon after our return to Alexandria, where to our great disappointment, after Christmas, we were again ordered to set up our H.Q., as it was thought that we needed someone more aggressive than 'Barmy' Morton to command our brigade.

In hospital I was treated for diphtheria and made to lie on my back and to keep as quiet and still as possible, as it affects the heart muscles and is sometimes fatal. However, my throat recovered and after a week or two I suggested that they might take some throat swabs and when they did, they found that I was free of that disease, but my high temperature and fever continued. So I was kept, supine, in hospital for a month and then sent on a month's sick leave, which I spent in Luxor and Aswan.

TRIPOLI

My long absence from the brigade was a great disappointment to me, more especially as they took part in an assault on the Dodecanese Islands. It was however an abject failure and our advance party, led by John Brocklebank, were treacherously handed over to the Germans by Greek partisans on the island of Leros – they became prisoners of war until it ended. If I had not been ill, I too would have been captured then.

While I was away on sick leave our Brigades had been told by G.H.Q., Middle East, to forward to them the names of barristers of more than ten years standing, and that included me. Therefore, when my leave was over, I was sent to the Legal Department of G.H.Q., Cairo to be Assistant Legal Advisor and I was promoted to the rank of Major. My Chief was an unusual old barrister, Colonel Eric Maxwell. Our job was to deal with the abstruse legal problems which arose through having to administer the conquered Italian territories of Eritrea, Cyrenaica and Tripolitania. It seemed to have little enough to do with the war, but it was interesting and demanding work. Having been thus employed from the summer of 1943 until spring 1944, I was appointed President of the British Military Court of Tripolitania, where I had to try local people - Arab, Berber, Italian and from a few other communities - for offences against our proclamations, and I had to try criminal cases if they involved racial conflict. I had had no previous judicial experience.

The Italian Judges, fine old lawyers in scarlet robes, were told that I was there to supervise them and to hear appeals from their decisions. I was only a thirty-five year old major, I looked much younger and I wore only khaki drill (cotton) uniform with shorts and my sleeves rolled up. The Judges were clearly surprised when they met me, but they co-operated splendidly. When trying inter-racial criminal cases I had to apply the Italian penal code, but I did not know Italian, and although I had an English translation of it and a fine interpreter, I decided to learn the language myself and persuaded the youngest of the judges to do exchange lessons with me. I taught him English and he taught me enough Italian to become, six months later, an army interpreter third class for which the army paid me £10 a year more!

Our courts were in what had been the Turkish and then the Italian Governor's Palace. I had Marshal Balbo's study as my office and the ballroom of the palace as my court. The work was strenuous – all the evidence given had to be translated into three languages: Italian, Arabic and English. This was because the advocates all spoke only Italian and the accused were mostly native Arabic speakers, who did not all speak Italian or English. This meant I had to record *all* the evidence in English as we were not provided with a stenographer. All the cases were fascinating – very few were for offences against our proclamations – they were mostly cases in which locals were accused of murdering, assaulting or defrauding Italians.

The most momentous case I tried, along with two British officers who were not lawyers, was one in which two brothers – desert Arabs – killed an Italian colonist's family on a remote plantation (to which we travelled) some seventy miles from Tripoli. Their defence was that one of them had been insulted by the withdrawal of the Italian father's promise to allow one of them to marry his daughter, which is a serious matter under traditional Arab custom. The trial took place at the small, remote town of Tarhuna and lasted a week. The court room was packed each day with locals wearing their long robes, which could conceal pistols and daggers. Scarcely any Italians attended the trial!

Before I gave our guilty judgement, which then carried the death penalty, we were advised by the British officer in charge of security to have our revolvers loaded and ready in case we had to shoot our way out of the nearest door in the court. However, it seemed that the Arabs were so impressed by our lengthy and painstaking display of British justice, that they accepted our verdict without protest. The death sentence, which we were obliged to impose under Italian law, was never carried out because the Italian parliament, after the liberation of Italy, decided to abolish capital punishment and the British Military Governor of Libya, Brigadier Travers Blackley, was ordered by HM Government to follow suit.

Tripolitania was a most interesting country, full of contrasting scenery; deserts, oases, lovely coasts, vast areas of vines and olive groves and Roman temples – especially at Leptis Magna and Sabratha. The Italians had done a tremendous amount to improve the country and reclaim it from the desert. One of the great joys for me was the plentiful supply of Arab horses to ride.

In April 1945 it became certain that the Germans would soon be defeated and that we would celebrate our victory with enthusiasm. It was the practice in Italy and her colonies to celebrate great national events by granting amnesties and reduced sentences to prisoners. As I had had the responsibility of sending a good many people to prison, it was decided that I should abandon my court work and consider the remission or reduction of the sentences of each of the several hundred prisoners in Tripolitania. Over the next two weeks I worked day and night examining the detailed records of each prisoner. The decision in each case was my sole responsibility and I was told by Colonel George Strickland, the brilliant Chief Legal Advisor, to err in favour of leniency. It was a formidable task and, as ordered, I completed it in time for VE Day on May 7th 1945, ending the war in Europe.

GOING HOME

Having been abroad for three years, I was keen to get home as quickly as possible. My father was ageing and in poor health and there would be a lot of work at the Bar after the war and I wanted to rebuild my practice before it was too late. There had not been a general election since 1935 and it was obvious that one would soon be held. The quickest way to get home from the Army, even for a short time, was to apply to become a candidate for Parliament, and if elected, one stayed home! But that was not my only reason for wanting to stand, and although it was traditional for barristers to take silk before entering Parliament, I knew that would take another five to ten years, which I felt would be too late to achieve much. The sooner I was elected the better it would be.

Through my parents I let it be known that I wished to be chosen as the National Liberal Candidate for the huge Dartford Division of Kent, which included Erith and Crayford as well as Dartford Rural District. The local Conservatives, as well as the National Liberals, wanted me and invited me to apply, so I flew home from Tripoli to my family home at Bridge House – what a thrill is was to see England again in May with the chestnuts in flower! My mother still looked young and beautiful, but my poor father had declined physically.

When I appeared before the selection committee I found that the Dartford people wanted me, but the Erith and Crayford people packed the meeting and wanted an industrialist as their candidate, so they chose a man called Ralph Grubb. He was heavily defeated at the poll, partly because at most of his meetings a heckler got up and shouted, "Luvverly Grub!" This was a phrase made famous by the wartime radio wit, Jimmy Hanley, whose son Jeremy became an M.P. and later Chairman of the Conservative Party.

CHAPTER 8

M.P. FOR HUNTINGDONSHIRE

I was waiting to return by air to Tripoli when National Liberal H.Q. invited me to go to Huntingdon (twenty-two miles from Oundle), where their chosen candidate had decided not to stand, when he found the constituency was too big for him. The County of Huntingdon is 365 square miles, eighty-one parishes, including four towns and some suburbs of Peterborough. The electorate, however, was only 39,000 people over twenty-one.

The prospect attracted me and I arrived on Monday, 8th June 1945, a carpetbagger in khaki, full of hope! The Selection Committee were six National Liberals and six Tories - the joint chairmen of the committee were a local landowner, Major Richard Proby (who had written the Conservative Farming Policy, which I had read on the train journey up there) and Sidney Peters, the retiring M.P., who was a local solicitor. They all lived to be over seventy and five of them lived to be ninety!

They had only one other applicant to interview - a surgeon wing commander in the R.A.F. with wings (a flying doctor). He was tall, dark and handsome and had a tremendous, magnificent blonde wife. I didn't think I had a chance and assumed that the committee would take one look at them, and choose him. But, to my surprise, they chose me - a

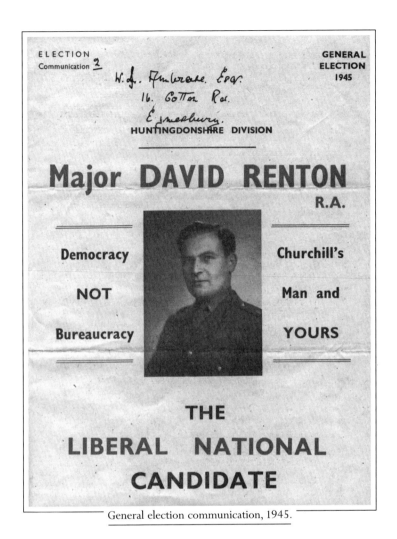

ELECTION
Communication 2

W.J. Amberede. Esq.
16. Cotton Rd.
E smeebury.

HUNTINGDONSHIRE DIVISION

GENERAL
ELECTION
1945

Major DAVID RENTON

R.A.

Democracy

NOT

Bureaucracy

Churchill's

Man and

YOURS

THE

LIBERAL NATIONAL

CANDIDATE

General election communication, 1945.

mere major and a bachelor - thanks to my grasp of the Conservative agriculture policy. When the Wing Commander was asked what the Conservative farm policy should be, he said "Oh, cheap food, cheap food, every time."

It was four days to polling day and I was a complete stranger. The Labour and Liberal candidates had already been beavering away on their campaigns for a week or more and they were younger than me, but had not served in the War. One of them was Harry Walston, a rich old Etonian and local farmer, who became a Liberal life peer many years later.

To make up for lost time, I had to "throw myself at the people." Few had motorcars but village bus services were good. Bus queues were captive audiences, and I spent most mornings in the towns addressing them. In the afternoons I drove at high speed visiting villages and hamlets. Every evening I addressed three of four well attended public meetings in towns or large villages.

There had not been a general election for ten years and locally the political parties had been inactive during the six years of war. We had no organisation, but wonderful volunteers. Most voters were not politically minded and many assumed that Winston Churchill would again be Prime Minister whatever the result. The campaign was an exhausting but thrilling experience.

Because most of our armed forces were still overseas, and the war against Japan was not over, there were three weeks between polling day on 5th July and the declaration on the 26th to enable service votes to arrive from all over the world. In those three weeks I had a glorious holiday: with my parents at Dartford and then in Scotland. That year I followed the strawberry season all the way from Cairo to Inverness, and the further north one went the better they were!

The night before the poll I stayed at the George Hotel, Huntingdon, and next morning when dashing to get to the count of votes in the Shire Hall by 9 a.m., I was nearly killed by a lorry as I struck a buttress of All Saints Church (where Oliver Cromwell was christened) – an accident caused by the narrowing of the pavement in that part of the street. Our result was:

Renton (Nat. Lib.)	15,389
Walters (Labour)	9,458
Walston (Liberal)	5,869
Majority	5,931

(I got only 62 more votes than my opponents.)

This good result encouraged me to think we had won nationally, but later that day it was a great shock to find there had been a Labour landslide:

(Photo © Cambridge Evening News)

My first grandson David shares our success after the 1974 election.

Labour	393
Conservative	212
Liberal	12
Independents	22
Speaker	1
Total	**640**

Becoming M.P. for Huntingdonshire was a great moment in my life. It was and is a lovely county – two-thirds undulating clay land and one-third flat fen, and river valleys. It had been a county since A.D. 921, when King Edward the Elder granted its first charter. The people were intensely loyal to its tradition and although it is only sixty to eighty miles from London, it had a feeling of remoteness. I sometimes came across people who had never been to London. The Cromwellian tradition of radical nonconformity still lived on among the older people. This small county had produced other famous figures of the past including, Samuel Pepys, the Earl of Sandwich, Nicholas Farrer, and the Dukes of Manchester.

I fought and won nine more General Elections there and remained the M.P. for Hunts for thirty-four years. Then I was followed by a much better Member, John Major, who became Prime Minister within just over eleven years, which was a record in the twentieth century. He and his wife Norma became very close friends, and we lived only two villages away from each other.

IN
OPPOSITION
1945-1951

Soon after being elected at Huntingdon I went home to Dartford until the assembly of Parliament on 1st August. That morning I got up early and drove to Westminster to make sure of getting a suitable seat. I was the first M.P. to arrive, and the front page of the *Evening Standard* had a photo of me arriving in my car. Having been brought up not to draw attention to myself, I was embarrassed by such publicity but soon learned to live with it!

Because the House of Commons chamber had been destroyed by enemy action, we first assembled in St Stephen's Hall. While we were waiting there to elect a Speaker, the Labour mob sang the Red Flag, which annoyed us - it revealed their revolutionary instincts. Then Winston entered, and we sang, "For he's a Jolly Good Fellow." Poor Winston: he did not expect to lose the election but from then on he dominated the Commons and bestrode the world.

On V-J Day, M.P.'s went in procession across the road to St Margaret's, the House of Commons church, for a thanksgiving service. Soon after that, those of us who were lucky in a ballot got tickets for the bar of the House of Lords to attend the state Opening of Parliament by King George VI. While we were waiting, Quintin Hogg asked me if I would care to practise in the chambers of Eric Sachs K.C., I was grateful and accepted at once because our pre-war chambers did not start up again as Roger Bacon became Chief Justice of Gibraltar.

I had not heard the King speak since hearing his very first public speech in January 1919, when he was Prince Albert, 'the flying prince', welcoming Alcock and Whitten Brown, the first men to fly the Atlantic. It was at Vickers Crayford where the aero-engines were made. He stammered then so badly that he took twenty minutes to make a six minute speech. Curing his stammer was a great achievement of that very fine King.

We came as a nation from victory in war to poverty and stagnation in peace. Because of the war we had no assets left overseas, but we had a sellers' world market and great opportunities. We could and should have done well, but the Labour Government made every imaginable mistake, including a massive programme of nationalisation. Their leader, Clement Attlee, was a 'Univ' man – he was kind, friendly, a moderate Fabian Socialist, modest and rather inaudible, but tough in dealings behind the scenes. Harold Wilson had been a Don at University College before the war.

In my election address I had said, "Having served in the Army throughout the war, I shall, of course, be especially keen to help ex-Service men and women to settle down on their return to normal life." Accordingly many of my questions and letters to ministers, and interventions in debate were attempts to help ex-service people. My father told me to remember that many men who had been wounded in the First World War had been patched hurriedly by surgeons in field hospitals, but they would feel the increasingly painful effects of it in later life. He therefore asked me to be sure to try and help them too.

Other matters I pursued in that first session related to food and agriculture, and to housing, of which there was a serious shortage. The first council houses to be built in the UK after the war were a pair at Kings Ripton, five miles from Huntingdon and a mile from Abbots Ripton (where I still live) and I accepted an invitation to open them in August 1945.

BACK TO THE BAR

I was released from the Army on 1st October 1945. The next day I did my first post-war case at the bar, at Huntingdonshire Quarter Session, defending the headmaster of a boy's home accused of stealing a watch from one of the boys. The foreman of the jury was that great novelist, David Garnet, whose book, *Aspects of Love*, is the basis of Andrew Lloyd Webber's musical. He spotted a flaw in the prosecution case before I did, and just as I was about to speak in defence, he stood up and suggested that the accused should be acquitted and he was!

There was plenty of work to be done in the Courts, including many divorce cases due to wartime separations and temptations and many men returning from the forces wanting to repossess their homes. For the first two years I did a lot of minor work, civil and criminal, much of it in Kent and East Anglia, but at last in 1948 more and better High Court work came my way, including substantial civil actions from two leading City solicitors' firms.

MAIDEN POST-WAR SPEECH

On the 26th October 1946 there was a debate on demobilisation. Winston Churchill spoke first for nearly an hour including interventions, then the Minister of Labour, George Isaacs spoke for the Government. I spoke three speeches after that. Although the unstable state of the world, and the danger of aggression by the Soviet Union, required us to keep large numbers of men overseas, I made a plea for the early release of those who, like myself, had been abroad for some years.

As soon as I sat down 'Hinch' (Viscount Hinchingbrooke, a constituent of mine) rose on a point of order. He said, "Speeches of great force and fluency are being made on matters relating to the War Office." He then complained that there was no War Office Minister on the Government front bench. Quintin Hogg then moved that the debate be adjourned, but this was not accepted by the chair.

A few days later as I rushed from court to the House to vote in division, I collided with the great Winston Churchill who had already voted. He threw his chest out and I bounced off it like a football! I said, "I'm sorry, Sir"; he replied, "That's alright, I saw you were travelling pretty fast and so I stopped. Go and vote!"

I was worried by the low standard of living and indeed by some real poverty among a small minority of the people of Huntingdonshire. That winter (1945-46) I therefore decided that I would take part in the debates on the three measures which implemented the Report by Sir William Beveridge (Master of 'Univ'). They were the National Insurance (Industrial Injuries) Bill, the National Insurance Bill and the National Health Service Bill. The Speaker called on me to open the debate on the third and last day of the second reading of the National Insurance Bill, which was a pleasant surprise and a useful opportunity. *(Hansard 11.2.46 cols. 37 to 40.)*

I started by saying that Beveridge had given hope to the men and women in the forces in the war: "... it made them feel that there was something further for which to win the war" and many of them said, "this will save a lot of worry." Then I criticised the Government's assumption written in the Bill, that 8 per cent of the work force would be unemployed when they had been promised full employment. I ended by saying, "...our greatness started with the Welsh Tudors and has continued ever since. Here in this National Insurance Bill we have an opportunity of joining together in advancing the social progress of the British people."

I served on the Standing Committees which considered each of those three measures, which all parties supported in principle, except that on our side we were worried about the way in which the voluntary hospitals and their funds were to be taken over by the State, and so we voted against the third reading of the National Health Service Bill. My father was worried by the way in which the medical profession were to become public servants as he thought they would lose their independence, and they would no longer be free to sell the goodwill on their own practices. One M.P. said "I'm the servant of my patient while I'm master of my fate but I'll be master of my patient as the servant of the State."

The result of all the legislation, of the nationalisation plans and of almost everything attempted by the Socialist government depended largely upon economic progress, which was non-existent, in spite of the sellers' market. The Government decided to apply for a huge loan of £1,000m from the United States, bearing 3 per cent interest and repayable at the yearly rate of £20m from 1951 until the end of the century. About one hundred of us in all parties were totally opposed to this and voted against it - we thought we should "pull ourselves up by our own bootstraps." Within a year or two the loan was frittered away through forced convertibility to other currencies, so it did us no good after all.

In the early autumn of 1946 I went on a small parliamentary delegation to Austria, which was divided into zones occupied by the USA, UK, France and the Soviet Union. Our main concerns were to see how our troops were coping with problems caused by the proximity of Soviet armed forces and to encourage the Austrians to recover from Nazism, revive their economy and re-establish democracy. Vienna itself was also divided into zones of each of the occupying powers. There and elsewhere in the Soviet zones we saw fine looking young Austrians in camps awaiting trial by a so-called 'People's Court', where they were quickly found guilty and sentenced to death.

In spite of having a busy round of visits each day, we were charmingly entertained in the evenings and once we went to the Opera. We were better fed then in Austria than in post-war Britain!

In early January 1947 it snowed hard and for six weeks we had continuous snow and ice. I still visited the constituency most weekends, held surgeries and got some skating on the flood meadows of the Great Ouse below St Ives. On weekdays court work and work in the House of Commons kept me continuously busy. The thaw came on 19th February and the rivers flooded furiously. In the late afternoon of Sunday the 22nd I drove across the 600 year old bridge from Huntingdon to Godmanchester, and the floodwater on the old North road almost covered the wheels of my car, which was the last to get through before the rising flood of the Great Ouse made it almost impossible to cross. I drove on to London, dined with Mrs Walter Duncan and her youngest daughter, Paddy, to whom that evening I became engaged. Wonderful! She had been christened Claire but, as her parents already had a son and two daughters and they had wanted another boy, she therefore became known for ever as Paddy - the next best thing! I was wonderfully lucky to be her husband.

TRANSPORT ACT: 1947

The government had announced in the King's Speech in November 1946 that they were going to nationalise the railways, canals, some bus services and long distance road haulage services. As I had worked in Paddington Station as a law pupil and had done so much work in the traffic courts as a barrister between 1934 and 1939, I naturally took an active part in the debates on the Transport Act. The Conservative Parliamentary Transport Committee was led by David Maxwell-Fyfe, and he and Peter Thorneycroft put up a stiff resistance to nationalisation. We were a well-knit team and, although we were heavily outnumbered on every vote, we made a strong impact. Peter's speeches were brilliant: forceful, fluent and witty. The Standing Committee, which considered the Bill, sat for two and a half hours nearly thirty times. I spoke there many times and Paddy often came and listened to our debates.

One of the many arguments we used against nationalisation was that it was irreversible. However, we did manage to denationalise buses, road haulage, and iron and steel, between 1951 and 1964, but until Margaret Thatcher became Prime Minister in 1979, nearly everyone assumed that nationalisation of the railways had come to stay. Now, however, privatisation is almost complete, thanks mainly to her.

17th July 1947.

OUR WEDDING

On 17th July, 1947 I married my beloved Paddy at St Margaret's Church Westminster. Her father, Walter Duncan had died in 1932 and she was given away by my friend John Grimston, her sister Marjorie's husband. The occasion was remembered because of the beauty of the bride, the flowers in St Margaret's and the amusing speech of my best man, John Boyd-Carpenter. The reception was at Dartmouth House, the club of the English Speaking Union, where my mother was a member.

For our honeymoon we went to Estoril in Portugal, which was blissful. Whilst we were there we were invited to call one morning on Prince Don Juan Carlos, who had become Pretender to the throne of Spain. He spoke good English, was well informed about our political situation and told us how much he liked and admired our country. While we were with him a small boy came into the room and rushed about - he is now the King of Spain and I cannot forget his first state visit to London because it was on 24th April 1986, the day my beloved Paddy died of cancer.

We had returned from our honeymoon in August 1947 and, as neither Parliament nor the courts were sitting, we did a round of visits: to my parents at Dartford, to the Inchiquinns in County Limerick, to the Gladstones in Dumfriesshire and to Kay Colquhoun, Paddy's sister and her husband Ivar at Luss, 'on the bonnie banks of Loch Lomond.' Then I went to Guildford to have my tonsils removed - very painful! My health improved greatly as a result.

On 28th September, I flew to Graz in Austria to defend a British Army officer at a court martial, on a charge of stealing petrol. The case lasted five days and he was found guilty. The Judge Advocate, Major Edward Blacklock (a Dumfries solicitor), told me before the case finished that he would next have to go to Venice and he kindly suggested I should go with him in his army car and that we should get our wives to join us there at the Hotel Royal Danieli, a lovely Renaissance building next to the Doge's Palace. When I mentioned to him my lack of foreign currency (which was quite a problem in those post-war years) and asked how our wives would manage, he said he would arrange for enough lire to be sent to an hotel in Milan for each of our wives. A day before his wife got there Paddy arrived and was handed all of the lire for both of them and she then went on to Venice. Next day, Mrs Blacklock arrived at the Milan hotel, asked for the lire and was told they had been handed the day before to *una bellissima bionda* (a most beautiful blonde). She wondered what her husband was up to, but she arrived in Venice and met Paddy and me with her husband and we all had an exuberant short weekend.

Paddy was fifteen years younger than me and marvellous at getting on with people of every kind - she was a superb M.P.'s wife. She told me many years later that I had proposed to her by asking her if she could bear to open a garden fete! For the last four years of the war she had been a VAD nurse, and after we went to live in Huntingdonshire in 1949, she joined the British Red Cross, and in 1954 she became the County President of the Red Cross - the youngest in the country.

In that autumn and winter 1947-48, life was hectic: in court, in a variety of my cases in out of the way places, weekend engagements in the constituency, speaking engagements at by-elections and the start of a new session of Parliament. We lived in London in my mother-in-law's flat in Cadogan Square until her large house in that square was derequisitioned early in 1949, when we moved into its two top floors.

In May 1948 my father died at the age of seventy-nine after a strenuous life, dedicated to his family and to his voluntary efforts in peacetime, including service on Kent County Council for eleven years. Holy Trinity Church at Dartford was completely full for his funeral and people stood in large numbers in silence as his funeral procession moved along the High Street. I know that, however hard I tried, I could not lead such a useful life as he had done.

In August 1948, Paddy and I had a much needed three week motoring holiday in France visiting: Peronne, Dijon, Menthon on Lac d'Annecy, St Raphael, Val d'Esquières, (where I started water-skiing), Pont du Card, Chaions and Boulogne. The French had completely recovered from the war and only petrol was rationed. While playing tennis at Menthon, a young Frenchman told us he had been to England that summer – I asked him whether he would soon make another visit but he replied, *"Non, monsieur on mange trop mal la bas!"*

Paddy was pregnant, but being bumped along hundreds of miles in my small car on French roads did her no harm, and in November she gave birth to Caroline, our flourishing, beautiful eldest daughter. A few

Dr Maurice Renton, my father, on his tennis court at The Bridge House.

days before she was born, Bob Hudson, who had been wartime Minister of Agriculture, addressed a crowded meeting of our farmers in St Ives Corn Exchange. In proposing a vote of thanks to him I said, "I am an over-expectant father and that is a very delicate and anxious condition for a man," whereupon all the farmers started laughing, cheering and stamping their feet!

Meanwhile my bar practice was steadily growing, especially in the High Court, which involved a lot of paperwork. However, it did not stop me from taking part in nearly thirty debates and asking over one hundred questions a session. Also, I became honorary Secretary of the Conservative Parliamentary Transport Committee, and continued to speak in transport debates. Peter Thorneycroft was our very effective chairman.

The Moat House, Abbots Ripton – my home since 1949.

THE MOAT HOUSE

Paddy and I had started to look for a house in Huntingdonshire and in March 1949, Ailwyn de Ramsey, a substantial landowner and Oundle contemporary, very kindly offered us a lease of the Moat House, Abbots Ripton, with ten acres and only five miles from Huntingdon, the centre of my large constituency.

I still live there. The house is 500 years old, but a fire in 1800 caused two-thirds of it to be rebuilt. It was originally a typical moated farmhouse enclosing about an acre of land, but a third of the moat has been filled in. The garden is charming and I have, for the past forty years, cultivated many roses, flowering shrubs and dahlias myself. There are masses of daffodils, and spring blossoms are abundant. It has a small orchard, mainly of apples. I was keen to keep a hunter there and Ailwyn was extremely helpful about it. For the next thirty years he kept a horse for me in his stable and it was ready groomed and saddled whenever I wanted to hunt or ride. I generally managed about twelve days hunting a season and on other days, he and I would ride around his farm, mostly on Saturday mornings, and in that way I learned a lot about farming. By buying horses cheaply, breeding from an old thoroughbred mare and, thanks to sharing a groom with Ailwyn, it did not cost me much.

The regular riding helped me to relax and keep fit after the demanding indoor life I led in Parliament and the courts on weekdays. I subscribed to the Fitzwilliam Hunt, which was mainly a farmers' hunt and its supporters were a relaxed and cheerful lot. To those who say that hunting is cruel, I must say that the foxes generally looked roguishly cheerful when being hunted, and I have never counted more than four seconds between the moment that the hounds closed in and the death of the fox. If hunting remains abolished, these foxes will suffer more by being killed by other more painful means.

At the hunt meet at the Moat House, c. 1965.

THE AA COMMITTEE

In May 1949, I was made a member of the Committee of the AA (The Automobile Association). The Chairman was Canon Hassard-Short, who had been vicar of one of the churches at Dartford and was in his late seventies. I was chosen, not because of that, but because of the interest I had shown in Parliament in getting roads improved and traffic moving! The Committee met only one morning a month and did a lot in three hours. In August 1950, Princess Anne was born and we made her our millionth member. The Duke of Edinburgh became our

President in 1952. He was brilliant: when presiding over our AGMs, he handled difficult questions most astutely, having thoroughly mastered the rules and the circumstances. I remained on the Committee until December 1955 and found it most interesting.

Aloft the shoulders of enthusiastic supporters after the 1952 election.

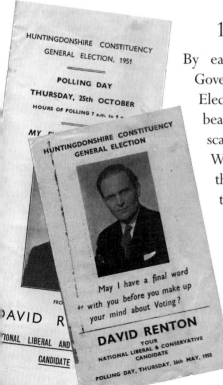

1950 GENERAL ELECTION

By early 1950, the fortunes of the Labour Government had sunk very low and in the General Election in February they might have been beaten, but the left-wing press raised a war-scare, suggesting that, if the Tories won with Winston as P.M., we would soon be at war with the Soviet Union. Although that was nonsense, the front page of the *Daily Mirror* on Polling Day had the headline "WHOSE FINGER ON THE TRIGGER?" This frightened enough voters in marginal constituencies, and so the Socialist Government got back, but with a majority of only seven seats, the lowest for one hundred years.

MISS ROBERTS

Soon after being re-elected for Hunts, I returned to my bar practice in the Temple. After I had worked at my arrears of paper work for several

After the 1956 election outside the Town Hall in Huntingdon.

days a good-looking young woman, whom I had never met, called to me in chambers: a Miss Roberts. She told me she had been the Conservative candidate at Dartford. She was the youngest in the country, and had greatly reduced the Labour majority. She asked me what one had to do to go to the bar and I told her she would have to join one of the four Inns of Court. "Which one?" she asked. When I modestly told her that I was a member of Lincoln's Inn, she said, "That's the one I will join," and she wagged her finger at me, not for the last time! There is now a historic document in the Inn: the application of a Miss Margaret Roberts to become a student there, sponsored by David Renton! She was amazingly self-confident and very charming. I did not know (but she may have worked it out) that twenty-nine years later, in 1979, I would become Treasurer of Lincoln's Inn, and she as Mrs Margaret Thatcher would become Prime Minister! And that in October 1979 I would have to preside over the best-attended dinner ever held in the Inn and propose a toast congratulating her.

1950-51 PARLIAMENT

In spite of their small majority, the Labour Government lasted until late 1951. Most of their legislation at that time was uncontroversial in principle but niggling in detail. They lost several divisions on minor issues. I continued to speak and ask questions about transport, agriculture, ex-servicemen and a variety of other matters.

We were still on short rations and the Government had tried to get people to eat food to which they were not accustomed. For example, snoek, which is not a reptile, but a fish which had hitherto been considered inedible! Whale meat was also advocated and when this was mentioned at Question Time, we were assured that careful palatability tests had been held. So I asked, "Who conducts these palatability tests? And do they have a whale of a time?"

On the 26th October 1950, King George VI opened the rebuilt House of Commons, which had been destroyed by German bombs in 1941. No monarch had attended the proceedings of the House since Charles I in 1639 tried to arrest five Members. The problem was overcome this time, however, by a splendid ceremony in Westminster Hall, when Douglas Clifton-Brown, the Speaker, presented the King with an address on our behalf, thanking him "for having caused the rebuilding, on the same site, of that Chamber in Your Palace of Westminster, which was allocated for the use of the Commons by Your Royal Predecessor Queen Victoria nearly a hundred years ago and which was destroyed by the malice of your enemies in 1941."

We knew that the Government could not last long with such a small majority and felt strongly that it was in the national interest to force them to hold another election as soon as possible. We therefore decided as a deliberate policy to harass them in the House of Commons, so much so that they would have to call another election before causing further damage to our economy. A group of us was formed, called the Active Back Benchers, with the specific purpose of keeping the House sitting late at night. Alan Lennox-Boyd was our inspiring chairman. One of our ploys was to oppose some of their numerous irksome orders and regulations.

The Moat House,
Abbots Ripton,
Huntingdon,
February, 1950.

TO THE ELECTORS OF HUNTINGDONSHIRE.

Ladies and Gentlemen,

It has been my proud privilege to be your Member of Parliament since July, 1945; and I wish to thank you for all your kindness and help, which have been a source of great encouragement to me.

Every one of you has an important part to play in the coming General Election, the result of which will reach far into the future of our country and the world. The issues this time are tremendous, for another instalment of Socialism like the last may bring us so near to the all-Socialist state that we could not afterwards restore freedom and save democracy—Liberalism would be destroyed and the trade unions seriously weakened.

I have always been a Liberal. Since 1931 I have considered that Conservatives and Liberals should work together for what is best in each of their great traditions, to ensure the survival of our 50 million people in this small island with an ever improving standard of living and to save liberty and democracy. The Conservative Party is now led by Mr. Winston Churchill, the greatest Englishman of our time, to whose Statesmanship Liberals as well as Conservatives owe so much. The Conservative Policy, with its aim of "a property owning democracy," is an enlightened and progressive one, which all true Liberals can warmly support. I am, therefore, standing as the National Liberal and Conservative candidate.

The Socialist policy of costly nationalisation, restrictive controls and high taxation has failed, in spite of enormous loans from U.S.A., gifts from our Dominions, and the 30 per cent. increase of production in private industry. Unless we regain our economic independence by June, 1952, when Marshall Aid ends, we shall not have full employment, or enough food. Devaluation, forced on us by the Government's incompetence, has made recovery more difficult and life more expensive. High taxation has increased the cost of living and reduced the true value of family allowances, pensions, wages and salaries, for the £ now buys 3s. 8d. less than in 1945. Food and Homes are still scarce in spite of the lavish promises made last time by Socialists.

We must have a change of Government and of policy, before it is too late. The policy I advocate is on the previous page. We need a Government which will give us strong leadership, inspire confidence at home and abroad, reduce taxation, restore the value of the £, and encourage our people to show what they can do by their enterprise and initiative.

My home is permanently in the County. If you again do me the honour of electing me to Parliament, I shall continue to help my constituents in any of their difficulties with the Central Government, help to improve the amenities of village life and make myself regularly accessible to you all.

Yours sincerely,

David Renton

General election leaflet letter for polling day Thursday 23rd February 1950.

At last in October 1951 that Parliament ended. In the general election that followed, with Winston Churchill still formidable as our leader at the age of seventy-seven, we won with a majority of only seventeen, even though we were on shorter rations after six years of Socialism than after six years of war. Our economy was stagnant; we had a housing shortage and the highest income tax in Western Europe. It was galling to see the contrast of the defeated West Germans repairing their buildings and rebuilding their economy faster that we did. They succeeded because the occupying Western Powers let them get on with it in a free economy without much regulation or control.

CHAPTER

10

WINSTON'S LAST GOVERNMENT 1951-1955

The Conservative and National Liberal Government had a formidable task.

In spite of our modest majority, the government lasted four and a half years and carried out a brave programme with a brilliant team, probably the most talented since the Liberal cabinet of 1906. The youngest member of the Cabinet was forty-two year-old Peter Thorneycroft at the Board of Trade, with whom I had worked closely in Opposition resisting the nationalisation of transport. Rab Butler was Chancellor of the Exchequer and reduced income tax in his first and second budgets and produced a rapidly improving economy. Harold Macmillan was Housing Minister and promoted the building of 300,000 houses in our third year. Alan Lennox-Boyd, whose Mid-Beds constituency was next door to mine, was Minister of Transport and piloted legislation to de-regulate nationalised buses and road haulage, in which I took part on the backbenches.

The Leader of the Commons, who also has to co-ordinate much of the Government policies, was that great wit and shrewd parliamentarian, Harry Cruikshank. He was asked whether the new government had found that their predecessors had left many skeletons in the cupboards of Whitehall. "Oh no!" he said, "They were hanging from the chandeliers." Of course there had to be one maverick: James Stuart, the wartime Chief Whip, who became Secretary of State for Scotland. When asked to "speak up" in a debate he said, "I'm most awfully sorry. I didn't know anyone was listening." But he got things done.

I was approached informally about becoming a junior minister but had to make it clear that my increasing family commitments (our second daughter, Clare, now wearing my wig at the bar, was born in August 1950) and the then small salary of a junior minister compelled me to continue to build my junior practice.

THE COUNCIL OF EUROPE

However, three weeks after the election I received a letter from the Prime Minister inviting me to be an alternate delegate to the Consultative Assembly of the Council of Europe at Strasbourg, which I attended from 4th to 11th December 1951. It was a genial short interlude in my hectic life. Ours was a friendly and thoughtful delegation, which included several of my close friends. The food and wines were a very acceptable change from the austerity at home.

I spoke at length in an interesting, but inconclusive debate on the draft European Convention on Human Rights. The Committee of Ministers had rejected a draft clause dealing with parent's rights with regard to their children's education, because they found it 'unworkable.' Continental lawyers at the Assembly considered that the Ministers counter-proposals were 'meaningless'. "In this case," I said, "I prefer the meaningless to the unworkable."

On my return from the first visit, when asked by the *Hunts Post* to give my impressions, I wrote:

I have long been convinced of the need for a European Consultative Assembly and greater cooperation between European Government; but I had never believed in European federation and still do not believe in it. Before I went to Strasbourg, I heard a variety of conflicting opinions among my political acquaintances about the interesting experiment, which is being made there. Some sceptics thought it was doomed to end and peter out in a cloud of disagreement over every important subject, including federation and the formation of a European army. Others, more helpful, said that the experiment was bound to succeed, in spite of disagreement, because no Western Government could afford to let it fail. My own conclusion was that the modest experiment was succeeding, in spite of the disagreement on the important matters and because of agreement on so many other matters, which were separately much less important, but which added up to an impressive total.

This was five years before the six-nation Treaty of Rome.

My only other visit to the European Assembly was from 15th to 23rd September 1952, and I took Paddy with me, which made it an even happier excursion. I was this time appointed to its Legal Affairs Committee. Monsieur Rolin, the Belgian lawyer who represented Iran in the dispute at the International Court at The Hague following the seizure in September 1951 by Iran of Abadan oil refinery, which belonged to the Anglo-Persian Oil Company, was deputed with me to draw up a constitution for a European Court of Human Rights. He worked on the French text using his knowledge of English and I worked on the English text using my rather rusty knowledge of French. It took us four days of uninterrupted careful concentration. We agreed the detail of each other's texts, which were approved by the Committee and eventually by the Assembly. When I returned to Westminster, Anthony Nutting, Under Secretary at the Foreign Office, asked me why the hell I had done it! He said it was not our policy to encourage such a Court but I pointed out to him that members of the European Assembly act on their own responsibility. I added that nobody had advised me against our having the Court, and I would have accepted such advice. Eventually the Cabinet decided to accept the Court's jurisdiction and many decisions have since been obtained there for and against the British Government. My wartime friend Vincent Evans (to whom I was best man at his wedding in January 1947) became a Judge of the Court after serving as Chief Legal Advisor to the Foreign Office.

One very hot and humid evening in mid summer 1952, when we were voting on a three line whip in large numbers, I decided to sit on a bench in the division lobby before voting, and Winston sat down beside me. I said, "You don't seem to mind the heat, Sir." He replied, "I've always enjoyed the hot weather but it's a most extraordinary thing that whenever British people have more than three days sunshine they say "when will the blazing skies relent?""

THE BRISTOL EXPLOSION ENQUIRY

From 1949 onwards I had been briefed by Shell-Mex and BP (then a consortium) to represent them in a number of planning inquiries in south-west England, where they wanted to build petrol stations and have them illuminated with advertising devices, mostly in open country. I told them that I was keen on preserving our lovely countryside, "Good!" said their solicitor, "That's why we want you to do these cases for us." It involved a lot of driving to visit the sites and attend the enquiries. I insisted they should modify some of their plans; otherwise we would have lost more cases than we did.

Then in mid-January 1952, they briefed me to appear in a most unusual and high-powered enquiry into a terrible explosion at a smallish garage at Bristol. In the basement were petrol storage tanks, which were old and leaking and gave off fumes. Repair work was done there, using blowlamps. One of the employees smoked continuously. The explosion took place when one of the Shell-Mex and BP petrol tankers were refuelling the underground tanks. The whole garage blew up and some neighbouring properties suffered damage. Eight people were killed including the driver of the petrol tanker.

The report of the Chief Metropolitan Magistrate, who held the enquiry at Bristol, concluded that every safety regulation concerned had been broken and blamed the local authority for failing to inspect the garage. His report became a bible on the subject.

On February 6th, I attended the Coroner's inquest at Bristol into the cause of death of those killed. At about 11am the Coroner announced that King George VI had died.

KING GEORGE VI

As I travelled back to London I could not help remembering the young Prince Albert's painful first speech which I heard in 1919; how he had served as a midshipman in the Battle of Jutland; how he had been the first royal air pilot; how diffident he was about becoming King; how he rose to the occasion in 1939 and how he and his wife Queen Elizabeth had shared with his subjects the dangers of the London blitz and so endeared themselves to the people.

On the 17th July 1952 our wedding anniversary, Paddy and I were presented to the young Queen Elizabeth for the first time. It was at a Buckingham Palace Garden Party. She was so natural and very friendly with everyone. When I told her I was M.P. for Huntingdon, she of course mentioned Oliver Cromwell, and I assured her that all my constituents were loyal to her. She jokingly expressed relief.

THE CORONATION 1953

The Queen's Coronation was the first great national event to be televised. The first TV set at Abbots Ripton belonged to our village post woman, Mrs Banister. Like her mother, she lived to be a hundred, although she used to deliver letters and parcels on her bicycle even when it was snowing. As I was allowed to take Paddy with me to the Abbey, Mrs Banister kindly had our daughters to her cottage to see the historic event on her TV. This is the account I wrote next day for the local press:

INSIDE THE ABBEY

BY DAVID RENTON, M.P. FOR HUNTS

Members of Parliament were 'commanded' to attend the Coronation, not because of any personal qualities we may possess but to represent our constituents. Our seats were in the South Transept in a gallery immediately above the Peers and with a full view of the Throne, but with no view of the Altar of the Chair of Estate.

Everything we saw and heard was equal to the greatness and dedication of our lovely young Queen, the ruler of the greatest concourse of nations and races in history: and she herself the descendant of sovereigns crowned in the same Abbey for a thousand years, the last twenty-eight of them in the same Chair placed on the same spot.

It was therefore meet and right that there should be Praise to God with the finest music; splendid robes and uniforms; effortless dignity in all who took part and a completely efficient organisation. These factors enhanced the deep religious meaning of the service, as well as its historical symbolism, and its message of hope for the future.

We had our best view of the Queen early in the Service, when she was presented as, "Your Undoubted Queen." She looked proud and modest, serene and sincere, as she stood there alone, and with thankfulness we shouted "God Save Queen Elizabeth." Very few people in the Abbey could see her between the Presentation and the Departure: but we heard her responses so clearly, and knew from them that she has purpose and courage, the will to serve her people, and a true belief in promises made to God.

Among other impressions of this greatest of days, we shall always remember the Archbishop's beautiful voice; the rippling waves of scarlet, ermine and diamonds as the peeresses curtsied; the endurance of the high officers of the Church and State (most of them elderly) who remained standing for nearly three hours without faltering; and Sir Winston Churchill in his Garter Robes, anxious to see more of the ceremony than was possible from his choir-stall.

Oliver Cromwell greatly admired Elizabeth I and his spirit may rejoice in Elizabeth II. His unworthy successor as Member for Hunts is grateful to his constituents for the honour of representing them. "We have seen the past: and it works." The future will now work even better.

(Photo © Lord Crathorne)

With The Rt. Hon. Sir Andrew Morritt, Vice Chancellor of the Supreme Court, at the "60 years in Silk" party in the the Lord Chancellor's Apartment in 2005.

TAKING SILK

The years from 1945 to 1954 were the most strenuous in my life. I had a very large rural constituency with many practical problems: the usual difficulties encountered by the farmers, many of them due to the weather; housing shortages; lack of electricity and of water supply in many villages; many children being educated at all age schools. There were many questions to be asked and speeches to be made in Parliament about those problems.

My varied practice in London, Kent, East Anglia and elsewhere involved a lot of travelling, as well as the mass of paperwork required of a junior with a High Court practice. I needed the income, especially as our family increased. The bar work interested me; it was often fascinating and always demanding. Parliamentary life as a backbencher was even more fascinating and meant a lot of late nights.

Being on the Committee of the AA was a pleasant contrast to parliamentary and legal work, and I also found it worthwhile to be on the Migration Council (for stimulating migration to the Commonwealth) and on the committee of the Anglo-Austrian Society.

In the Commons I was elected Chairman of the Conservative backbench Transport Committee in 1953. We had weekly meetings and supported the efforts of our Ministers, Alan Lennox-Boyd and then John Boyd-Carpenter, to undo some of the harm done by nationalisation of transport. Several transport Bills each year claimed my attention. I served on the Statutory Instruments Committee, which always had a big agenda and I became chairman of the House of Commons Branch of the British Legion.

There were many weekend speeches to be made, but life at the Moat House with Paddy was so blissful that I managed to keep more or less sane. Riding and gardening were a necessary tonic.

At Christmas 1953, Eric Sachs became a High Court judge, and Quintin Hogg having moved elsewhere, I became head of chambers while still a junior. When I applied early in 1954 to become a Q.C., it was, thank goodness, granted and life became more rational. It meant fewer but better cases, scarcely any paperwork and, at first, a drop in income.

At the head of the list of twenty-two silks that year was Ronnie Armstrong-Jones, aged fifty-eight, a hard working and popular member of our South-Eastern Circuit, whose son Tony, later married Princess Margaret, our Royal Bencher at Lincoln's Inn whom I got to know well. I was at the age of forty-five almost the youngest person in the list of Q.C.'s.

On 13th September 1954 our third and youngest daughter, Davina, was born. It eventually became apparent that she was severely handicapped, mentally and physically. Twenty-four years later I became Chairman of MENCAP.

Davina's Christening on 22nd November, 1954, with Caroline left, and Clare.

(Photo © Universal Pictorial Press & Agency)

WINSTON CHURCHILL RESIGNS

After the Coronation, Winston had a slight stroke, but during the recess he recovered well enough to carry on as Prime Minister. In fact his old exuberant spirit returned and, although he lightened his load, he delivered some pretty stimulating speeches - especially on defence and world affairs. He resigned on 31st March 1955, without ceremony but with the satisfaction of knowing that he had 'set the people free', improved their standard of living and made the world more peaceful for the time being.

Anthony Eden, on becoming Prime Minister, called a general election in May which we, the Conservatives and National Liberals, won with a majority of twenty-eight. The Liberals won only six seats. It was the only election in the post-war era in which the winning party won more than half the votes polled.

ROADS AND TRAFFIC IN THE USA

The Committee of the AA was anxious to get motorways built and wanted more off-street parking. They decided to send me to the United States with their Touring Manager, Ronald Cann-Evans, to discover what progress was being made there in improving the road systems, to examine their multi-storey car parks and parking meters, and to find out how it was all financed.

I took Paddy with me. Neither of us had been to the United States before, although her mother was from Boston, where one of my father's elder brothers, Julian, (an Edinburgh lawyer) had been Head of the Highways Department. He invented 'the Renton Cauldron' for spreading hot tar on roads.

We flew to Boston on 26th August 1955 and were welcomed by the President of the first of the five American motoring organizations, who carefully arranged our four weeks tour. Nearly all our journeys were on magnificent highways. We travelled about 2,000 miles in Cadillacs, accompanied by two delightful experts: Bill Canning and Mac Adams.

Addressing the American Automobile Association, 1955.

After taking stock of the traffic arrangements in Boston, and meeting the Head of the Traffic Department, we had the joy of being driven through Maine, New Hampshire and Vermont: lovely, lush, hilly country in which the attractive colonial architecture of New England is so well preserved. Then we stayed a couple of days at Albany, the capital of New York State (but hundreds of miles north of New York City). We called on Governor Averill Harriman, who wanted to hear about Winston in retirement.

Then we went on to Buffalo on Lake Erie, whose outflow is over Niagara Falls and into Lake Ontario. We walked along the platform between the falling water and the rock, over which it falls and roars as it hits the pool below. Very exciting!

At Toronto, the Vice-President of the Ontario Motor League, who rejoiced in the name of Warren Hastings, welcomed us. (His namesake's trial in Westminster Hall was the longest in our own history, seven years, and is marked by a brass tablet on the floor). We found that Toronto on a Sunday was very austere: no alcohol in our hotel!

On we drove through Southern Ontario, a great fruit growing area – it was harvest time and the fruit was delicious. We crossed back into the USA at Marine City and went to Detroit, where we stayed at the Dearborn Inn, close to the Ford Motor Museum. We toured the vast factory where Ford cars were being turned out rapidly.

The long journey from Detroit to Chicago, 287 miles, included a stop at Kalamazoo where a glamorous blonde called Pearl filled our petrol tank! This inspired Ronald, Bill and Mac to compose a poem during the last stage of our day's journey:

> *From Kalamazoo to Timbuktu*
> *The girls are the nation's pride,*
> *But hear of a girl of the name of Pearl*
> *And let this be your guide.*
>
> *From County Cork to Old New York*
> *I looked for a peacheroo,*
> *And from coast to coast the only toast*
> *Was Pearl of Kalamazoo.*
>
> *So I started to woo in Kalamazoo*
> *While I still had a packet of dough,*
> *But she turned me down for an Oshkoah Clown*
> *And I had to watch her go.*
>
> *My grief I'd hide in suicide*
> *But it seems so awfully risky,*
> *So starting tomorrow I'll drown my sorrow*
> *In a bath of Bourbon whisky.*

Chicago was amazing. Everything was on a vast scale: the skyscrapers, the crowds, the volume of traffic, the car parks, the cattle market, the hospitality and the drinking. It was and is one of the largest commercial and industrial cities in the world. (When I went there again, twenty-one years later, there was still more of everything!)

On the Lake-side Drive we saw a system for varying the number of traffic lanes for use in each direction, according to the volume of traffic. That road has eight lanes and could be divided into four each way, or six one-way and two the other, by mechanical mobile dividing stripes. Maintenance of the hydraulic machinery, which works them, is a serious problem, however, and it did not always function when needed.

Our next journey was by air to Louisville, Kentucky, where their 'Derby' is held. We stayed the night there before motoring to Lexington in the Bluegrass Country, which is famous for its thoroughbred bloodstock. The whole of Kentucky seemed to be dedicated to racing thoroughbreds.

Then by air to Pittsburgh, a vast steel-manufacturing city built among several hills. It had the most difficult traffic problems of all and was chaotic. At one heavily congested part of the city there were five layers of traffic lanes, built over each other.

The climax of our tour was our visit to Washington DC: spacious, long avenues, neo-classical, grand architecture; no traffic problems but lots of discussion with traffic experts at Federal level and wonderful hospitality especially by the 'Three As' – the American Automobile Association.

Then to Annapolis, the US Naval Academy where we called on Admiral Boone, the Principal - austere, tall, unsmiling and impressive. At Philadelphia, we had the thrill of visiting the room in which the Declaration of Independence was signed.

Our final visit was to New York, which was certainly not planned for the convenience of motorists and was the only place where we found aggressiveness between motorists, police and public. My wartime friend, Vincent Evans, who later became Chief Legal Adviser to the Foreign Office, was attending the United Nations Assembly and invited us to the Opening Session.

On 21st September, we left New York on board the *Queen Mary*. After our hectic, revealing, enjoyable, but exhausting tour it was good to have five days at sea to recover in the luxury of that great ship. During the voyage, Ronald and I prepared the first draft of our report which we divided into six parts:

1. The American Problem.
2. Road Development Policy.
3. Road Safety.
4. Technicalities of Road Construction and Traffic Control.
5. Parking and Parking Meters.
6. Vehicle Inspection.

In the past forty years there have been so many road developments both in the United States and in our country, that there is now no advantage in describing our many conclusions and recommendations – but I am glad to say that our report was well received and nearly all our recommendations were put into practice here within a few years. Our AA President, Prince Philip, held a private meeting with us to discuss our findings, and a few days later his Private Secretary, General 'Boy' Browning, wrote a most appreciative letter about our draft report, which was later printed and widely circulated.

On Tuesday December 20th, Paddy and I took Ronald Cann-Evans out to dinner at a restaurant. Luckily, my mother had asked, "Which one?" The Chief Whip tried telephoning me, then her, to ask me to telephone Anthony Eden, who was ill in bed at 10 Downing Street. I did so, and he asked me if I would go to the Ministry of Fuel and Power with Aubrey Jones, who was three years younger than me and became an M.P. five years later than I did, but he had the advantage of being the son of a coal miner and had a fine academic record. I wasn't sure whether I was to be the Minister or the Parliamentary Secretary, so after thanking him, I asked for time to consider the matter and let him know in the morning. When he said he had to get the list out that night, I weakly agreed to serve. Next morning I found I was to be the junior minister!

CHAPTER 11

FUEL
AND
POWER
1956-1958

On arriving at the Ministry of Fuel and Power (as it was then called) at Thames House, Millbank, just before Christmas 1955, I was greeted at the entrance by Sir John Maud, the top civil servant there, who had been Dean of 'Univ' in my last year.

Thus began two eventful, varied and interesting years as Parliamentary Secretary to the newest government department, which was responsible for the nationalised coal, gas and electricity industries, and for supplies of oil and petrol. I knew too little about coalmining, but Aubrey Jones, our Minister, was not only the son of a Welsh miner, well educated, urbane and gentle and a graduate of the London School of Economics. All his decisions were right and he was quietly efficient, but his personal relationships were not always easy - especially with a group of right wing Tory M.P's, known as 'the fuel furies'. They included Colonel 'Juby' Lancaster, a former coal owner, 'Hinch' (my friend and constituent, Viscount Hinchingbrooke), Angus Maude and especially Gerald Nabarro, a vibrant and self-assertive character from the West Midlands.

MALENKOV

One of my early duties as a junior minister was a strange and unexpected one. When Stalin died, in 1953, nobody had been chosen to succeed him but after a bit of dithering, the Russian Politburo appointed Georgi Malenkov as Prime Minister. He had been Stalin's henchman and helped him to carry out some of his massive massacres. Two years later, Kruschev forced Malenkov's resignation and transferred him to be Minister for Power Stations.

Before that happened Lord Citrine, the left-wing Chairman of the Central Electricity Authority, had invited a deputation of Soviet power station chiefs to visit the UK to see our modern power stations: coal fired, oil-fired, hydro-electric and even our first nuclear power station at Calder Hall.

Malenkov decided to lead the Delegation and this put our Foreign Office into a flat spin. Not wishing to offend Bulganin, who had succeeded Malenkov, or Kruschev, by then the dominant member of the Politburo, the Foreign Office advised that Georgi should not be given top level recognition, but that he could be received by the Junior Minister. It therefore fell to me to welcome him at the reception given for him at Lancaster House on his arrival in London. I was told that, although, being middle class, he had been brought up to speak French, I was not to speak it with him but that a Russian interpreter (a member of their Embassy staff) would always be on hand.

He was cheerful and relaxed and wanted to know my views about nationalisation. When I told him I had voted against it but now had to help make it work, he said jokingly that that would not be difficult! When the Soviet Ambassador joined our conversation, Malenkov looked worried – even frightened – and ceased to converse freely.

Citrine insisted, in spite of Foreign Office advice, that Aubrey Jones should receive Malenkov and his deputation privately before and after their tour of our power stations, which lasted about fifteen days. The Ambassador attended both of those meetings and Malenkov was clearly anxious not to say anything that might put himself out of favour with the Politburo. When Aubrey asked him several times to give us his impressions of his tour, which included the Scottish Highlands, Georgi merely said, "There has been a lot of work."

A farewell dinner was given for him at the Connaught Hotel, where the food and wines were splendid. Malenkov sat between Citrine and me, with the interpreter sitting behind us. The Ambassador was on the other side of Citrine, and so could not hear my conversation with Georgi who thus became relaxed. He said what a beautiful country we had and how much he had enjoyed the tour. He also told me how much he liked the red Burgundy with the meat course, a Gevrey Chambertin, 1947 - so I told the wine waiter to keep filling his glass. He became really cheerful and voluble and when we talked about horses he told me that in the Russian revolution, when he was a teenager, he had ridden in a Cossack regiment.

Two years after his return to Russia, he was involved in a failed coup against Kruschev and ceased to be Minister for Power Stations. In 1961 he was expelled from the Communist Party, became 'a non-person' and was never heard of again.

THE MINERS

We depended economically on the effort of the 700,000 miners in over 300 mines to produce enough coal for industry, railways and ships, and to keep the home fires burning. Whenever the miners went on strike for higher wages, the economy was at risk and their leaders knew it. North Sea oil and gas had not yet been discovered but we imported oil increasingly from the Middle East. Nuclear power was in its infancy and it would take some years to make a major contribution, if any, to our ever-growing needs.

As Parliamentary Secretary I was responsible, among other things, for health and safety in mines and quarries, and so I went down about a dozen coalmines in various parts of the country. Having stayed the night before in a nearby hotel, I would generally arrive early at the manager's office and put on overalls and a helmet in time to go down the mine with the morning shift at 8am. When we reached the foot of the mineshaft we generally had a long walk to the coalface, where we often had to crouch down because some of the coal seams and the galleries were only about five feet high. Nearly all coal extraction had by this time been mechanised by using various coal cutting methods, such as circular saws carried on large machines, which moved forward or sideways as the coalface was cut away. The noise of these machines made conversation difficult. The coal was loaded into trucks on narrow gauge electric railways – pit ponies having recently been freed from life underground, thank goodness!

At the end of the shift I always had a pithead shower and lunch with the miners in their canteen. Although I was to them just a right-wing junior minister, the miners nearly always gave me a most friendly welcome. In South Wales they wanted to talk about rugby and in Nottingham about cricket. The only area where I was unwelcome was South Yorkshire, which twenty years later became 'Scargill country'. There one could cut the atmosphere with a knife, possibly because they had memories of being ill-treated by the coal owners.

The lives of the miners were dirty, dark and dangerous. In 1956, my first year of responsibility for their safety, fifteen miners were killed in two separate explosions. It was the lowest number on record, but of course we claimed no credit for it. It was mainly due to the vigorous steps taken after nationalisation in 1947 to increase safety in coalmines, and to the disciplining of the mines by enforcing them to comply with safety procedures.

Part of my responsibility was as Chairman of the National Joint Pneumoconiosis Committee, whose job it was to reduce miners' deaths caused by inhaling coal-dust. The main cause of this problem was dust inhaled after 'shot firing' explosions, which blast the way underground to create galleries or tunnels. The rule was that after each shot was fired, the small team doing it should keep away from the scene of the explosion until the dust had settled which took at least twenty minutes. As the men were paid according to progress made, however, they often disobeyed that rule so as to earn more money, and thus they inhaled the

Going down the mines Nottingham,1957.

dust and died from the irreparable damage caused to their lungs. There was a special wing at Cardiff Hospital for miners suffering from pneumoconiosis. When I visited them there, strongly built men in their thirties on their deathbeds, several would admit that they knew the risk they were taking by disobeying the rules and said it was their own fault, but the employers should have done more to protect them from their folly.

Although coal mining was better paid than most other manual work, it seemed a terrible way of life - one wondered why men went on doing it. The reason was that most mining communities were in remote places, where not much other work was available and was less well paid than mining. As the standard of living for most people was steadily improving, I wondered how much longer men would go on descending into the bowels of the earth, risking their health and their lives in such an unpleasant and dangerous occupation. They were nevertheless proud of their achievements - a pride which descended from father to son in mining families for generations. So they took it all for granted. The mining M.P.'s, mostly supported by the National Union of Miners, were a cheerful lot and I got on well with them.

Now that few men are required for that awful way of life, we should be thankful that our own country's prosperity no longer depends upon it to such a great extent as it had done ever since the start of the industrial revolution in the eighteenth century.

CLEAN AIR ACT 1956

The old habit of burning raw bituminous coal in open fireplaces everywhere and in factories, railway engines and ships caused appalling air pollution in towns and cities, where at least 80 per cent of the population lived and many suffered ill health as a result. The smogs were mainly caused by all these coal fires, especially in winter. At the Smithfield Show in December 1954 about a third of the cattle died from it.

In North West Kent, where my home had been until I married in 1947, we had the biggest concentration of cement factories in the world and they created a further problem. Four million tons of cement was produced there, and in one month it had been estimated that 105 tons of cement dust had fallen onto one square mile.

Previous legislation had dealt, to a limited extent, with industrial pollution and there was an Alkali Inspector with the power to enforce it. Those further problems had to be tackled, however, and Gerald Nabarro had in 1954 tried to do so with a Private Members Bill, which the Government did not accept, but in November 1955 they introduced their own Bill. It prohibited the emission of dark smoke from any chimney, required new furnaces to be smokeless so far as practicable, required the emission of grit and dust to be minimised and enabled local authorities to create smoke control zones in which it would be an offence to emit dark smoke from any building. This meant that only smokeless fuels, such as coke, Welsh steam coal and phurnacite, could be used in fireplaces. As every miner was entitled to a ton of free coal a year, mining members strongly opposed this proposal but they were voted down.

The Clean Air Bill was introduced by Bill Deedes, then Parliamentary Secretary to the Ministry of Housing and Local government, on behalf of his Minister, Duncan Sandys, who replied to the second reading debate. By the time the Bill reached Standing Committee, Enoch Powell had succeeded Bill Deedes. I was brought in mainly to deal with the availability of smokeless fuels. A good right-wing effort!

Within about six years, the Bill was mainly implemented, with immensely beneficial effects on the health and happiness of the nation. Indeed it was one of the best measures in the last century for people's health but our leaders made no effort to claim credit for it.

SUEZ

In late July 1956 Colonel Nasser, President of Egypt, announced that he had nationalised the Suez Canal Company. It was from the start in 1868 under Anglo-French control. By the end of October attempts to persuade Nasser to accept an international consortium to control the canal had failed, and the British and French Government sent a large and powerfully armed force to capture Port Said and take possession of the Canal. Egyptian military resistance was ineffective but they closed the Canal by sinking several ships in it. As a result, our vital oil supplies from Iran and the Gulf States were seriously interrupted. Bringing the oil round the Cape meant long delays and increased costs. Our oil reserves would not last more than a few weeks. Our best hope was to try to obtain more oil from Texas and Venezuela, but that too would have meant more delay because disused oil wells would have had to be reopened, and anyway not enough tankers were readily available.

In mid-December 1956 we therefore had to re-introduce petrol rationing, which had ended in 1950. Luckily we still had millions of petrol coupons left over from that time, but the Treasury refused to let us have enough money to administer effectively a fair and comprehensive scheme. In quickly setting up regional petroleum offices we had a stupendously difficult job. We had to answer many questions and there were several debates about the imperfect working of the rationing scheme and the increased costs of production and of living. It lasted until mid-May 1957.

EDEN'S RESIGNATION: MACMILLAN BECOMES PRIME MINISTER

Eden had for some years been troubled by ill health and even at the height of the Suez crisis he had flown to Jamaica for a short rest cure. On 9th January 1957 he resigned and the Tory party went into a short state of turmoil about who should succeed him. Rab Butler was his Deputy P.M. but had been a reluctant dragon over Suez. Macmillan, in Eden's absence, had been resolute and unequivocal. The Queen was therefore advised to send for Macmillan, who immediately showed himself to be the man to rise to the occasion.

Among the changes he made was the appointment to the Cabinet of Percy, Lord Mills, as Minister of Power in place of Aubrey Jones. The P.M. asked me to stay on as the junior minister in the newly named Department, but as my new Minister was in The Lords, there was a lot to be done in the Commons, including several major Bills, so the P.M. arranged that Reggie Maudling, Paymaster General, should help in the Commons without having any responsibilities in the Ministry. (This was because Reggie had also been appointed to negotiate our entry into the European Free Trade Area, which never occurred).

It was an unusual arrangement but it worked perfectly, mainly because Reggie, besides having a brilliant mind, was marvellous to work with: good-humoured, patient and understanding. I also got on well enough with Percy Mills, who delegated freely and let one get on with the job.

The legislation which Reggie and I had to pilot through the House of Commons was non-controversial in broad principles but it was lengthy and very technical, and much of the detail gave rise to controversial discussion. The Electricity Bill came first.

REORGANISATION OF NATIONALISED ELECTRICITY

When the Labour Government nationalised the fuel power industries between 1946 and 1950, we used the argument that there should not be any nationalisation because once it had taken place denationalisation could not be achieved. However, we decided that the Central Electricity Authority, which was responsible for generating and distributing electricity, was over-centralised, and so in December 1956 we introduced a Bill to create a separate Generating Board, and to have electricity distributed by Area Board in England and Wales. An Electricity Council would advise the Minister, and "provide and assist the maintenance and development by Electricity Boards in England and Wales of an efficient, co-ordinated and economical system of Electricity Supply." This reorganisation was a real improvement.

MINING SUBSIDENCE

Throughout the coal-mining areas considerable damage was often caused by subsidence of land. Compensation was not always paid to those who suffered, and anyway payment of it was often delayed. In the discussions on the Bill, which we introduced in January 1957, the main controversy was about "who should bear the cost of paying compensation." We said that the National Coal Board should do so, as they normally had to do under our Common Law. Our Bill, for the first time in our history, provided a remedy of compensation or repair for damage caused by mining subsidence.

OPENCAST COALMINES

As we had decided to introduce a Bill in 1958 to regulate opencast coalmining, I thought I ought to go and see how it was done without spoiling the rural environment. Removal of a big depth of topsoil, extracting the coal and several years later replacing the topsoil, so that farming could be resumed, was the massive task to be achieved.

In early January 1958, I visited several opencast sites in Northumberland, and was impressed by the efficiency displayed. Although the dislocation was unsightly whilst the coal was being extracted, the restoration of the land was impressive at the two sites I visited. During my stay in the area, I also went and saw some 'drift mines' - with entrances on the sides of hills and a short walk down to the coalface. They were owned, not by the National Coal Board, but by small partnerships of working miners.

When I had been up there for two days and was having lunch near an open cast site, a message came from Whitehall telling me to go to London at once to see the Home Secretary. I took a fast train South and went straight to see Rab Butler, who was deputising as P.M. for Harold Macmillan, who had gone to Australia and New Zealand, having had to appoint a new Treasury team after the resignation of Peter Thorneycroft as Chancellor of the Exchequer, and his colleagues, Nigel Bird and Enoch Powell. "A little local difficulty," Harold called it.

As Jack Simon Q.C. had been appointed Financial Secretary to the Treasury, Rab had to find an Under-Secretary to replace him at the Home Office. Before inviting me he asked me whether I agreed with the Wolfenden Report, which recommended getting prostitutes off the streets and legalising homosexuality between men over twenty-one. I agreed with the former, but had strong reservations about the latter, and feared that legalising it would create problems in the Armed Forces.

CHAPTER 12

THE HOME OFFICE AND RAB 1958-1962

The Home Office is our oldest Government department. It was the original department of State and it still has a wide range of responsibilities. Indeed it is obliged to handle any matter that has not been allocated to any other department.

When I arrived there in early January 1958, it was still in Whitehall near the Cenotaph. I found that my responsibilities as Under-Secretary of State were wide and varied. They included the Constitution, North Ireland (which still had its own government at Stormont), the Channel Isles and the Isle of Man: Law and Order; the Police, Probation Officers, Prisons; Fire Services, Civil Defence; Charities, Betting and Gaming, Cruelty to Animals and various other matters. The other Under-Secretary was Pamela Hornby-Smith, but she was not given so much responsibility. I was there from January 1958 to July 1962.

Rab Butler was Home Secretary from 1956 to 1962, and he always had other responsibilities - there was no office of Deputy Prime Minister, but he was in fact Harold Macmillan's Deputy. Rab was also leader of the House of Commons, Chairman of the Conservative Research Department and he had a large and busy constituency in Essex. He therefore had to delegate much of his Home Office work to me and much less to Pam, who was not a lawyer.

We did not get a Minister of State in the House Office until after the General Election of 1959, when Dennis Vosper was appointed. When Rab delegated, he did so freely and confidently and did not fuss. If one of us was challenged, he simply assumed that we were right and defended us without hesitation. This made him a splendid chief to work with.

On my table, when I arrived at the Home Office in January 1958, there were four Bills, which we had to get through the Commons by Easter and somehow we did! I had whole or main responsibility for: the Isle of Man Bill, the Recreational Charities Bill, the Life Peerages Bill, and the House of Commons (Redistribution of Seats) Bill.

Because he was so busy with his responsibilities outside the Home Office, Rab never served on a Standing Committee on Legislation, to which most Bills referred, and he did the minimum on Bills taken on the floor of the Commons. As a result one had to pilot much of the legislation single-handed, but sometimes with the valuable help of a Law Officer.

THE LIFE PEERAGES ACT 1958

This was a one page Act that gave power to the Queen (on the advice of the Prime Minister) to confer baronies for life upon men and women. The Labour Party opposed it. My only task was to speak against an amendment, which would have limited the number of life peers to one hundred at any time. Our purpose was, as I said, "to enable distinguished people to become peers without their having to become hereditary peers." (Hansard, 25th March 1958.)

The reason I gave for not agreeing to a limit of one hundred was that "...it would be illogical as well as anomalous to limit the number of life peers while there is no limit to the number of hereditary peers!" I added that the limit would give the 900 hereditary peers a huge majority!

There are now about 450 life peers and I was thrilled when I was made a Life Peer in 1979 on the advice of Margaret Thatcher, after being M.P. for Huntingdonshire for thirty-four years.

STREET OFFENCES ACT, 1959

Prostitution is the oldest profession. By 1959 legislation was imperative to tackle the problem of streetwalkers. Our Bill was intended to strike a blow at pimps who exploited the women and at 'kerb crawlers.' Following vigorous debate the Bill passed, with slight amendment. It stood the test of time well bearing in mind the need to reexamine the entire problem periodically in the light of changing social conditions.

COMMONWEALTH IMMIGRANTS ACT, 1962

By 1961 there was a consensus that that we were an overcrowded island and that it was essential for the good of people already here that we limit the number of immigrants from the Commonwealth.

When the first Commonwealth Immigrants Bill was introduced to Parliament after lengthy consultation it caused a storm in its passage through the House at various stages.

The Labour Party opposed the Bill passionately. Rab Butler asked me to pilot the Standing Committee stage. There was such a commotion at one stage the speaker had to adjourn the House.

Eventually the Bill reached the Statute book largely in the form we had proposed at the outset and was the first of many enactments restricting immigration.

UK REPRESENTATIVE AT THE FIRST CONFERENCE OF EUROPEAN MINISTERS OF JUSTICE

In our constitution we have no Minister of Justice, although most European countries do have one. In May, 1961, there was held in Paris the first ever conference of European Ministers of Justice, and strangely enough I was appointed to represent the United Kingdom, although I was merely a Home Office Under-Secretary. Lengthy discussions took place without any important decisions being reached.

CHAPTER

13

FROM MINISTER BACK TO THE BAR AND THE BACKBENCHES

In July 1962, Harold Macmillan was under pressure from some of his younger Cabinet Ministers to make major changes in the Government. By then I was nearly fifty-four and had been in Government for six and a half years, and he sent for me. He told me that after my four and a half years in the Home Office, although he felt I had done well, he had no other appointment for me, but hoped to have me back in Government at some future date - I always doubted that, and it never happened! However, he said I was to become a Privy Councillor and I was so appointed.

BACK TO THE BAR

So I returned to practice at the Bar. My previous practice had gone to other Q.C.'s, and so getting going again after six and a half years was a slow process. However, it did happen over time and I became busy in practice, was given a lot of part time judicial work and some backbench legal responsibilities in the Commons. My old Chambers had been split and no longer existed but I was invited to join other chambers, where I was the senior Q.C., but not the head. Slowly a fresh practice grew and became varied - about half of it being criminal work, which was easy and sometimes exciting.

In January 1963, I became Recorder of Rochester for five years. It was only a few miles from Dartford, my birthplace. Rochester is an ancient and historic Cathedral city, easy to reach by train from London and I was delighted to become its 'Second Citizen' after the Mayor. Most of Chatham Dockyard, which was in my jurisdiction, was still very active and at first produced many of the cases I tried. Some of the younger dockers had a habit of getting drunk and using their fists. The barrister who most often appeared before me was the splendid young Patrick Mayhew, who many years later became Attorney General, and then Northern Ireland Minister in Cabinet. After being at Rochester for five interesting years, I was appointed in 1968 Recorder of Guildford, where most of the criminals were different; and drugs and fraud were the most frequent offences.

I also sat as a part time relief judge for two years at the Old Bailey, where a large proportion of the men I tried were from abroad.

(Photo © Feature Press Photo Agency)

Outside Buckingham Palace after being knighted by the
Queen, 1964. With Paddy and Clare.

CHAPTER

14

DELEGATIONS TO AUSTRALIA AND ELSEWHERE

In the early autumn of 1965, when our Courts were in its recess, I was appointed Deputy Leader of a Parliamentary Delegation to Australia. The original leader of it was a senior Labour M.P. who was a Privy Councillor, but he fell ill when we reached Central Australia and so I had to take over from him.

We landed in the tropical Northern Territory and stayed at Darwin for a few days. It was very hot, humid and sparsely populated and we were taken by car to various places on the northern coast, where we had the thrill of seeing crocodiles and sharks.

Then we went to the centre of Australia, which was similarly hot, very dry and had few human inhabitants. The small British community there welcomed us and drove us to visit several very large nearby farms. Next we flew to Adelaide, a splendidly built seaport on a large estuary, the capital town of South Australia.

DELEGATION TO GUYANA

In September 1968, I was made leader of a Parliamentary Delegation to Guyana, formerly known as British Guiana, where my mother was born on 28th November 1885, on my grandfather's sugar plantation near

Georgetown, the capital. Soon after she was born there my grandfather's health needed attention, and so he took his family with him by sea to London, where he got medical advice to leave British Guiana and move to a drier climate. They moved to Alexandria in Egypt, where my grandmother, although British, had lived as a girl. Ironically my grandfather, on his return to British Guiana to make arrangements for the move to Alexandria, sold his plantation to Quintin Hogg, who was a well-known local financier, a family friend and the grandfather of my great friend, also Quintin Hogg, who became Lord Chancellor. The site of the old plantation is now occupied by Georgetown University. So my grandparents sailed to Alexandria in Egypt and landed there on my lovely mother's first birthday. In spite of having crossed the Atlantic three times before her first birthday, my mother lived to the ripe old age of ninety-three!

Four generations, at David's christening outside the Crypt of the House of Commons 1970. My mother, Eszma (Tumpsey) DL-MR, David Douglas Dodds-Parker and Caroline.

(Photo © Keystone Press Agency Ltd)

Our delegation greatly enjoyed our visit to Guyana, where we were sent to celebrate the country's independence. It was a fascinating place with lovely scenery, ancient British buildings and a racial mixture of native people, of Indian immigrants, of descendants of West African slaves, and of families of British early settlers. They seemed to get on well together, and when we were invited to attend a celebration in their new Parliament, at which I gave an encouraging address, they seemed to be united and so they remained.

After that Parliamentary ceremony we travelled up country and onto the border with Venezuela where we saw the deepest waterfall in the world, Kaieteur, covered by a river, which springs from the massive Potaro River (400 feet wide).

RETURN HOME

My practice grew steadily and it included the longest case I ever had: defending in a long term fraud case at Chelmsford Assizes in 1963. There were thousands of pounds at issue, and my client was convicted on the basis of a paper trail that he had left behind him. I had to advise that there was no hope of a successful appeal.

ROYAL COMMISSION OF THE CONSTITUTION

In 1971, Selwyn Lloyd became Speaker of the House of Commons and thus ceased to be a Member of a Royal Commission on the Constitution, which was a necessary requirement to advise on whether there should be devolution (responsibility for internal self-government) for Scotland, Wales and Northern Ireland. I was therefore appointed to fill the vacancy caused by Selwyn's appointment. I was the only member of the Royal Commission opposed to devolution of Scotland and Wales, but I did think that it was worth considering for Northern Ireland.

CHAPTER

15

THE
RENTON
REPORT

In 1973, I was made Chairman of the first official enquiry since 1870 to consider how Acts of Parliament should be drafted. It was called the Committee on the Preparation of Legislation, but became known as The Renton Report. Among our members were distinguished lawyers and experienced politicians under my chairmanship: The Duke of Atholl, The Rt. Hon. Baroness Bacon, The Hon. Mr Justice Cooke, Sir Basil Engholm, Mr J A R Finlay, Sir John Gibson, Mr P O Henderson, Sir Noel Hutton, Mr K R Mackenzie, Sir Patrick Macrory and Mr Ewan Stewart.

Our statutes had become much too detailed and lengthy, mainly because they attempted to cover every hypothetical situation that might arise, instead of enacting broad statements of principle, which for centuries had been the usual practice. Of course legislation dealing with taxation or defining criminal penalties had always had to be detailed, but there was no need for that in most of our legislation. The Committee made 121 recommendations and conclusions, of which 89, if accepted, would have involved material change.

When our Report was debated in 1975 in each House of Parliament, it was welcomed. It soon became apparent, however, that Civil Servants and Parliamentary draftsmen did not want to have to define statements of principle, but wanted to cover every detailed situation which might arise. In the thirty years since then the drafting of Statutes has varied, but in recent years it has become usual to express too much hypothetical detail.

In 1978, the Statute Law Society produced a report on drafting, which did not have official authority and unfortunately ignored much of our advice.

END OF BAR PRACTICE

The Royal Commission, the two year's work on The Renton Report, and increased Parliamentary duties compelled me to retire from my bar practice in 1974, when I was sixty-six. Luckily the ancient rule that on retirement a barrister's fees are not taxed was still in operation! Having in thirty years become one of the most senior M.P.'s I was appointed, in the House of Commons, to the Committee of Privileges.

CHAPTER

16

A VARIED
LIFE
1979
ONWARDS

Entering the House of Lords with my sponsors
Lord Allen of Abbeydale and Lord De Ramsey.

BECOMING A PEER

In April 1979, the Labour Government with Jim Callaghan as Prime
Minister held a general election, which the Conservatives won by

seventy seats. Margaret Thatcher, who became the first woman to be Prime Minister, had tried to persuade me at the age of seventy to remain in the Commons, where I had been by that stage, for thirty-four years, but I refused and so she said, "I shall want you in the Lords." So I became a life peer in July 1979.

Having been Chairman of The Renton Committee, I was asked to keep in close touch with several ministers on the drafting of Conservative Government Bills, and did so. However, it was not easy to get Government officials or parliamentary draftsmen to alter and improve the draft Bills which came before Ministers. Eventually they obliged and for several years the legislation did show some improvement.

Paddy with Davina in 1967.

HRH Queen Elizabeth and Brian Rix, 1981.

MENCAP

Because of my disabled youngest daughter, Davina, I became closely involved with MENCAP (then the National Society for Mentally Handicapped Children) in 1970 when, anticipating the Education

(Handicapped Children) Act, I chaired the Society's Education Panel, and in co-operation with the Westhill College of Education in Birmingham, we devised a Special Needs Training Course, which became the blueprint for all such courses in the UK. As the Act made it possible for 'mentally handicapped' children to be part of the education system, it was both urgent and necessary to ensure that sufficient teachers became available to teach those with special educational needs.

Seven years later, at the end of 1977, Lord Segal retired as Chairman of MENCAP and I succeeded him. I remained Chairman until 1982, when I was succeeded by Lord Allen of Abbeydale. I then became the first ever President of MENCAP (the acronym had been adopted in 1979) and remained as such until making way for Lord Allen in the spring of 1998. Sir Brian Rix (as he then was) followed Lord Allen as Chairman and remained so for ten years. He then became President and Philip Allen and I took a back seat as Past Presidents! However, my interest in MENCAP continues to this day.

In 1981, Brian Rix suggested that we became a 'Royal' society and I approached my old friend Willie Whitelaw, who was then Home Secretary, and persuaded him that such an honour would enhance MENCAP's standing in the world, as well as the adults and children that the society served. Her Majesty the Queen gladly gave her approval and we became the Royal Society for Mentally Handicapped Children & Adults. At the turn of the century, this title was considered to be somewhat cumbersome and old-fashioned, so it was shortened and approved as the Royal Mencap Society by our Patron, Her Majesty Queen Elizabeth the Queen Mother, shortly before she died. However, in spite of having such a splendid formal title, our Royal Society continues to be called MENCAP in everyday use.

I often say that perhaps the best thing I did for MENCAP, in the middle of my term as Chairman, was to get Brian Rix, the famous comic actor, made Secretary-General. He did the work superbly, increased the revenue and improved the administration. He served in this role for seven years before coming Chairman. Lord Allen and I had the great pleasure of introducing him to the House of Lords as a Life

With HRH Queen Elizabeth and Paddy at MENCAP, 10th December 1981.

With Davina on August 12th 1998, my 90th birthday.

Peer in 1992, since when he has regularly attended the Lords and continually takes part in debates affecting 'mentally handicapped people', who for some years now have been labelled as 'people with a learning disability'.

My poor little Davina, now aged fifty-one, still unable to walk or talk and without any improvement in her condition, has been the main reason for my continued interest in the world of 'learning disability'. I love her and visit her every two or three weeks at Ravenswood, the splendid village community in South East Berkshire where she and many others are cared for.

Lincoln's Inn 1979. DL-MR seated centre.

LINCOLN'S INN

In January 1979, I became Treasurer of Lincoln's Inn for twelve months. This means being chairman of the Inn, and it involves plenty of work and much responsibility. Having retired from the Bar in 1974, and ceased to be M.P. in April 1979, I was free to concentrate on the Treasurer's duties. The poor financial state of the Inn, which is about 600 years old, was my main concern, however, it gradually improved and a few years later we again became solvent. Paddy and I had lived in the Inn for several years, which was a great advantage to me as Treasurer.

GRAND NIGHTS

Twice a year we held major dinners, to which a number of distinguished guests are invited, and which our Royal Bencher, then Princess Margaret, generally attended. She was a diligent Royal Bencher, was interested in the Inn, and was excellent in welcoming students from the Commonwealth, of whom we had a steady flow of about thirty a year.

When, alas, Princess Margaret died in 2002, we invited the Duke of Kent to be our Royal Bencher, and he accepted, attends regularly and shows much interest in the Inn.

Prince Richard, Duke of Gloucester, attended one of my Grand Nights and enjoyed it, although being a teetotal, he was not stimulated by our splendid wines!

At Grand nights we have no speeches.

INDIA

In February 1980, Paddy and I visited India for the first time and travelled about the country for three weeks. Her father's family, the Duncan's from Scotland, had thrived in India since about 1850, first as tea planters in Assam and then as 'Duncan Brothers of Calcutta', a prosperous firm of exporters which still thrives, but which is now part of a much larger trading conglomerate. After India became independent, the last Chairman of Duncan Brothers was Paddy's only brother, Athol, who in the Second World War served in the British Army, and won the M.C. in Burma. By the time that Paddy and I visited India, he had retired and, with his wife Seynolda Butler, returned to live in England. We therefore did not visit Calcutta, but we enjoyed visiting Delhi.

MEMORIES OF HUNTINGDONSHIRE

When I was first elected M.P. for Huntingdonshire in 1945 my majority was 6000, and in each of my ten General Elections I never had a majority of less that 5000. My best majority was 10,002 in the February

(Photo © Cambridge Evening News)

Victory after the 1974 general election. Outside the Town Hall with Paddy.

1974 election. Paddy and I were the two, and if we had not been so over zealous it would have been a nice round figure of 10,000! In 1945 there were only 39,000 voters over twenty-one and at the time of my last election in 1975 there were 93,000 voters over eighteen. The huge increase was mainly due to the influx of people from North London as part of the post-war policy to move people away from poor housing in London, which enabled Huntingdon, St Neots and St Ives each to absorb several thousand more people, for which they were paid considerable sums by the Treasury. Many of the larger villages also increased their populations naturally and without Treasury help!

Owing to the great increase in population Huntingdonshire was divided into two constituencies soon after John Major became M.P. and his new constituency covered, broadly, the western half, including Huntingdon, Godmanchester, St Ives, St Neots and Elton. John was a splendid and delightful successor to me from 1979 to 2001 and he and his wife Norma have had for many years a charming country house and garden only about a mile from Huntingdon. He is now President of the Huntingdon Constituency Conservative Association, of which I have been the Patron for some years, and is a brilliant public speaker.

In spite in the increase in its population over the years, the constituency has remained mainly unspoilt, indeed it has retained its character and its party political composition has not changed, partly because many of its new inhabitants became Conservatives! It is a very friendly place and although it is basically Conservative, party politics do not play a prominent part in people's lives there or in local government.

I grew to love the area and have now been resident there for fifty-seven years.

In pensive mood, 1978.

(Photo © Cambridge Evening News)

DRIVING TEST AGED 94

At the age of ninety-four, I became one of the oldest people in Britain to pass my driving test for the first time. When I first learnt to drive, driving tests were not a legal requirement, which continued until 1934. I decided to finally bite the bullet and take the test after 'a minor altercation with a wing mirror', when driving on the Embankment in London. The DVLA said that they could not remember an older successful candidate; only four men over seventy had passed the test in 2002, even though twenty-four applied. There are no official figures for nonagenarians!

THE HOUSE OF LORDS

When I became a life peer in 1979 it was easy for me to choose a title as I was the first Renton! Some years later my friend, and a very distant kinsman, Tim Renton M.P. was made a life peer and became Lord Renton of Mount Harry, which is on the South Downs in Sussex.

There were about 450 life peers in the Lords when I joined and well over 900 hereditary peers, of whom several hundred attended from time to time and voted. However, only about 100 of them were regular attendees and in 1999 the current Labour Government persuaded both Houses that the 920 hereditary peers should elect 92 from their number who alone would have the right to attend the House of Lords and vote. They are a useful group, numbering many people of ability, talent and valuable experience. The number of life peers has steadily increased and most of them have a variety of parliamentary and other experience. Some of the Labour life peers, however, were appointed simply because of their work for their party and without serving as M.P.'s.

Of course, the Bishops and the Law Lords have for many generations made a valuable contribution to our debates, and it is tragic that the Law Lords are being removed from our House because their advanced legal experience is an important contribution to our legislation.

The family at the Moat House to celebrate my 80th birthday, August 12th, 1988.
Back: David Dodds-Parker and Maxim Parr. Seated Caroline, DL-MR, Amelia Scott, Clare.
Front: Helen Scott, Duncan Scott.

To my surprise, in 1980 I was elected Deputy Speaker of the House and remained so for five years, when I decided that I had presided for a few hours every week for long enough and so gave it up. Deputy Speakers have no power to intervene and correct peers speeches, but merely have to announce the items of business and debate, including divisions.

In the past fifteen years the quality of membership of the Commons has declined and that of the Lords has improved. From early times the Commons had no less than twenty Q.C.'s and sometimes up to thirty or so, plus members of every profession, senior, retired and members of the Armed Forces, business people, farmers and others making up a valuable cross section of our society. Membership of the backbenches was originally intended to allow them to carry on with

(Photo © Ken Challenger / The Hunts Post)

My 95th birthday celebrations with many friends in The Town Hall, Huntingdon.
My daughters, Caroline Stanley and Clare Scott are immediately behind myself and
Lady Thatcher, seated.

their real occupations; now however, they are expected to spend the
majority of their time in the Commons when the House is sitting. As a
result many M.P.'s are less experienced and now there are only ten
Q.C.'s there, eight of whom are Conservatives.

In the Lords we have thirty-four Q.C.'s of various ages and in all
parties, many of whom are still in practice. The Lords, although
not elected but appointed, is in some ways more representative of
influential occupations than the Commons.

Until July 2005, when I was ninety-six, I played an active part in
debates in the Lords. In 1998 I had been, to my surprise, unanimously
elected President for Life of the Conservative Peers Association and a
member of the Executive of our backbench members. I enjoyed that
and took part in debates while being so.

During the long vacation in August 2005 I fell ill and was in
hospital for four days; my balance deteriorated and my memory began

to decline. I had already resigned as President for Life of the Conservativ Peers Association and this took effect from October 2005.

With Jonathan Djanogly M.P., Lady Thatcher and Baroness Emily Blatch.

Dancing with Margaret Thatcher at my 90th birthday celebrations.

Also in the summer of 2005 the office of the Library of the House of Lords drew attention to the fact that I had spent sixty years altogether in Parliament – thirty-four years in the Commons and twenty-six in the Lords – and that nobody else had been in both Houses for sixty years since 1900. It is now sixty-one years!

How lucky I have been!